Development and implementation of the EU grand strategies:
sociological, policy, and regional considerations of Agenda 2030

Tamara Besednjak Valič, Victor Cepoi, Erika Džajić Uršič,
Urška Fric, Cristian Gangaliuc, Alenka Pandiloska Jurak,
Borut Rončević

Development and implementation of the EU grand strategies: sociological, policy, and regional considerations of Agenda 2030

**Bibliographic Information published by the
Deutsche Nationalbibliothek**

The Deutsche Nationalbibliothek lists this publication in the Deutsche Nationalbibliografie; detailed bibliographic data is available online at http://dnb.d-nb.de.

Library of Congress Cataloging-in-Publication Data
A CIP catalog record for this book has been applied for at the Library of Congress.

This book was financially supported by Erasmus+ Jean Monnet Activities, Jean Monnet Centers of Excellence. Project Title: Strategic Observatory for Europe 2030. Project number: 611564-EPP-1-2019-1-SI-EPPJMO-CoE / Grant Decision no. 2019-1810/001 / Grant Agreement/Decision Nr 2019 - 1810 / 001 – 001.

More information on SOE2030 project is available on: https:// www.eu2 030.eu/

The European Commission's support for the production of this publication does not constitute an endorsement of the contents, which reflect the views only of the authors, and the Commission cannot be held responsible for any use which may be made of the information contained therein.

This publication has been edited by Borut Rončević and Petra Kleindienst.

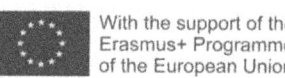

ISBN 978-3-631-88676-2 (Print)
E-ISBN 978-3-631-89428-6 (E-PDF)
E-ISBN 978-3-631-89429-3 (E-PUB)
10.3726/b20448

Open Access: This work is licensed under a Creative Commons Attribution CC-BY 4.0 license. To view a copy of this license, visit https://creativecommons.org/licenses/by/4.0/

© Tamara Besednjak Valič, Victor Cepoi, Erika Džajić Uršič, Urška Fric, Cristian Gangaliuc, Alenka Pandilos-ka Jurak, Borut Rončević, 2023

Peter Lang – Berlin · Bern · Bruxelles · New York · Oxford · Warszawa · Wien
This publication has been peer reviewed.
www.peterlang.com

Table of contents

List of tables 9

1. Introduction 13

Part I. Setting up the strategic observatory for Europe 2030

2. The EU regional policy in the light of its past, present and future 19
   What is a region? 19
   The policy formulation 20
   Cohesion policy historic development 22
   What lays ahead 26
   Governance, impact, and evaluation 27

3. Discourses swirling the implementation of the grand strategies: Case of New Industrial Strategy 33
   Industry; a yes or a no? 34
   Industry – the back bone of the EU and the question of re-industrialisation 39
   European approaches towards industrial policies in search for their efficiency 41
   Making sure the New Industrial Strategy 2030 works 43

4. How consistent is the EU policy? From formulation to assessment and evaluation. The case of research and innovation 47
   The innovation policy overview 49
   Setting up the context 50
   Getting to know the 3O's strategy 54

The innovation assessment tool 56
Comparing the 3O's strategy and the European Innovation Scoreboard ... 58

Part II. Achieving the 2030 sustainability goals: Case studies

5. UN sustainable development goals 2030: Industrial symbiosis within the European policy assessments 69

   Policies towards concept of the Industrial Symbiosis 70

   Policy development 71

   Industrial Symbiosis as a tool in the middle 73

   The EU sustainable recovery towards Industrial Symbiosis concept 76

   EU existing sustainable indicators 80

   EU funding systems towards sustainable developments 82

6. Investing in the European Union economy – a focus on recovery policies for Romania 85

   The socio-economic development in the European Union 87

   Regional Cohesion Policy 87

   Romania 88

   Recovery plan 89

   Recovery plan in action 91

   Business support, research, development and innovation 93

   Innovation – a bridging point for Romania's Recovery Plan 94

   Innovation and Recovery Plan 96

   Streamline governance of research, development and innovation 96

   Enhanced cooperation between business and research 97

   Support to integrate the research, development and innovation organisations in Romania in the European Research Area 97

   Private sector aid schemes 98

Establishment and operationalisation of Centres of Competence 99

Development of a programme to attract highly specialised human resources from abroad in research, development and innovation activities .. 99

7. Open innovation towards EU's Green Deal circular economy goals: Can the Covid-19 epidemic be an opportunity to accelerate the achievement of goals? 101

   The timeline of circular economy legislation and actions: From the beginning to nowadays 103

   The timeline of open innovation legislation and actions: From the beginning to nowadays 106

8. Conclusions 111

References 119

About the Authors 137

List of tables

Table 1:	Abbreviations	11
Table 2:	The EU Cohesion policies in data	22
Table 3:	The EU membership	23
Table 4:	EU Region development level	28
Table 5:	GDP per capita as indicator of development	35
Table 6:	Shares of GDP in industry among selected European countries	36
Table 7:	Employed in industry; percentage of total employed	38
Table 8:	Innovation Scoreboard Comparison	59
Table 9:	The Comparative Table of 3O'S Strategy and EIS	62
Table 10:	Roadmap of EU policy documents	77

Table 1: Abbreviations

CE – Circular Economy	NGEU – NextGenerationEU
EEA – European Environment Agency Indicators	NRRP – National Recovery and Resilience Plan
EGD – European Green Deal	RED – Renewable Energy Directive
EIP – Eco Industrial Park	REG – Regulatory-based measures scenario
EP – European Parliament	
EU – European Union	RES – Renewable energy source
EUR – Euro	SCP – Sustainable Consumption and Production Indicators
GDP – Gross Domestic Product	
GHG – Greenhouse Gas	SD – Sustainable Development
IE – Industrial Ecology	SDG – Sustainable Development Goals
IS – Industrial Symbiosis	SDI – Sustainable Development Indicators
SDGI – Sustainable Development Goal Indicators	
	SDS – Sustainable Development Strategy
MS EU – Member States of the European Union	SI – Structural Indicators
	UN – United Nations

1. Introduction

The subject of this book are the challenging and exciting issues of the implementation of the European Union's grand strategies, with a particular interest in the implementation of the current Agenda 2030 and its Sustainable Development Goals. We see this as particularly exciting, both as a research topic and as a policy issue. This is not only due to the almost proverbial difficulties in implementing the joint strategy in a union of 27 very diverse countries, a union where the key institutions in spite of decades-long institutional development still lack the power – and the budget – relatively equivalent to those of the nation states. The really interesting fact is that Agenda 2030, unlike the Lisbon strategy and Europe 2020 is not a grand strategy developed for the European Union, but a document developed and accepted by the United Nations, albeit with a very significant impact of the European Union. In this process the European Union has recognised the fact that many of the major issues that the EU is facing are global in their nature and should be tackled not only by the European Union, but also beyond its borders, on a global scale. Some of the global issues with a profound impact on the European Union are the climate change, illegal migration and, not least, war in Ukraine, which is impacting the European and global energy market, food supplies, and perhaps also leading to reorganisation of global geopolitical alliances, as well as the flows of energy, food, industrial components etc. Some of the challenges have such a strong short-term impact, that already accepted strategic priorities and decisions are being questioned and re-examined, for example the decision of Germany to close nuclear power plants and scale down the coal-powered power plants.

The implementation of the EU grand strategies is a phenomenon that has already been the subject of intense interest by both researchers and policymaker (Makarovič, Šušteršič, and Rončević 2014; Haverland and Romeijn 2007; Borghetto and Franchino 2010). The most researched is the Lisbon strategy, which concluded in 2010. However, a significant number of publications on the impact of Europe 2020 already exists (Stec and Grzebyk 2018; Makarovič, Šušteršič, and Rončević 2014). This research points to significant discrepancies in implementation among the Member States. Some of the divisions are between Northern and Western Member States on one hand and Eastern and Southern ones on the other (Wüst and Rogge 2022; Kasprzyk and Wojnar 2021), but others may be discovered, and the reasons for them could be unveiled in the future research.

One possible approach in this research is the Cultural Political Economy (CPE) approach, based on evolutionary mechanisms of variation, selection, and retention of dominant discourses (Jessop 2004; 2010; Jessop and Oosterlynck 2008), as well as on mechanisms of selectivities (Sum and Jessop 2013). This has already been used in research on implementation of Europe 2020 (B. Rončević and Besednjak Valič 2022). It was also the theoretical foundation of Jean Monnet Centre of Excellence "Strategic Observatory for Europe 2030" (SOE2030), the result of which is this volume.

This is the first effort to scratch the surface of the implementation of The Agenda 2030 with CPE, although more systematic research is yet to follow, especially on the basis of data collected during the SOE2030.

Chapter 2 addresses the following:

To improve the economic well-being of regions in the European Union, the EU sets the regional policy also referred to as Cohesion Policy. It intends to avoid regional disparities by boosting regions, that are lacking behind. The aim of this chapter is to enlighten the changing policy throughout history and how it developed into the present. We will be considering, how the priorities changed, how it is supported by the budget and which mechanisms are available for funding. Researching the current Cohesion Policy shows a quite complex approach not fully transparent to an ordinary EU citizen. While reading the EU Strategy, which sets six Commission priorities for 2019–2024, the regional aspect is not clear and unambiguous. Namely, it is not the EU Strategy, that sets the regional development course but rather the regional development supports the EU Strategy selected indicators.

Chapter 3 addresses the following:

It was a Lisbon treaty to determine the primary goal of the EU to become: "the most competitive and dynamic knowledge-based economy in the world, capable of sustainable economic growth with more and better jobs and greater social cohesion". Since the Lisbon Treaty, the Europe 2020 was adopted, and nowadays Agenda 2030 is working towards the same goal. However, since the time of the Lisbon Treaty, several global events and processes have taken place – from the global crisis in 2008 to Covid-19 pandemics in 2020 and the Russian invasion of Ukraine in 2022. Nowadays, the New Industrial Strategy is only a part of the Agenda 2030. Still, it follows the aim to deliver the twin transitions: make the EU industry more competitive globally and enhance Europe's strategic autonomy. The present contributions will discuss the narratives and statuses surrounding individual groups of EU countries with respect to reaching the goals of the New industry Strategy. Special attention will be posed to questions of technology transfer and protection of intellectual property as two of the tools to contribute toward the goals of the New Industry Strategy.

Chapter 4 addresses the following:

Innovation was not introduced in the latest formulation of the European Commission's priorities for 2019–2024. However, it remains an important Policy Area and an impactful tool for achieving the newest goals. The chapter focuses on analysing whether the existing strategies are compatible with the assessment methodologies used by the EU. For this purpose, the study will compare the parameters within the Research and Innovation policy area and the European (Regional) Innovation Scoreboard. The first aim is to observe how the tool represents the policy goals. And the second is to assess the validity of the Scoreboard to analyse policy impact. The study's relevance is to highlight the auto-evaluation potential of the EU.

Chapter 5 addresses the following:

This chapter analyses the state of the art of recent developments in the EU's policies and strategies for implementing the Industrial Symbiosis as a goal of the European Green Deal. The European Commission has been monitoring Industrial Symbiosis in Europe, reflecting a range of facets of dropping the cost by treating waste, dropping landfill resources, new deals produced, consequences for environmental nonconformity, destruction and waste management and economic benefits. The present chapter explore the priorities of the Industrial Symbiosis development of EU as part of the grand strategic visions till 2030, properties and lessons learned from strategy and implementation of the policy formulation as a mechanism of European Union vision selection. The preliminary research question of the chapter is identifying, if the European Union programmes still support enough the improvement of Industrial Symbiosis in the European Union?

Chapter 6 addresses the following:

The Covid-19 health crisis and the ongoing Russian-Ukrainian war have left significant impact on the economic development of the European country members. As a result, in order to balance the overcome of the crises, the European Union has reshaped how does it understand and mitigate these crises that occur or will occur on the European continent. The aim of the chapter is to focus on the analysis of the European Union support for recovery policies, with a specific emphasize on aspects as research, innovation and digitalization and SMEs. These two are among the strategic investments priorities that the EU has in its InvestEU Programme. Additionally, the chapter will focus on aspects as innovation activities, transfer of technologies, support of business, collaboration of enterprises. The results, will lead not only to the examination of the above-mentioned crises' consequences, but also to a better understanding of challenges to economic and social sustainable transitions.

Chapter 7 addresses the following:

The chapter presents the status quo of the EU's Green Deal circular economy goals. More specifically, it provides a comparison of achieved goals before and during the Covid-19 epidemic. In the chapter, open innovation and circular economy are dealt with as two closely-related paradigms where both represent actions under an ambitious EU policy – open innovation as one of the actions for shaping Europe's digital future, and circular economy as one of the actions for a cleaner and more competitive Europe. Both present the prospects for Europe 2030 and still require research and discussions – although some of them already exist. The chapter includes timeline overview summarizing EU's ambitious policy; leading indicators explaining efforts of the EU; budget support and mechanisms for funding before and during the Covid-19 epidemic. In its core, the chapter deals with the question whether the Covid-19 epidemic can serve as an opportunity to accelerate the achievement of goals.

Last but not least, this book is intended to have both academic impact and also educational impact, so it will cater to the interest of both EU studies researchers and teachers, students of EU studies, policy-makers, as well as the general publics. The book will deal with insufficiently explored area of the EU studies, namely the formulation and implementation of long-term strategies of the European Union. The book will be of a particular importance to the academics working with Cultural Political Economy approach. For the it will be the demonstration of analytical robustness of this approach and original contribution in terms of data collection protocols for this particular approach.

The book is coming at a time, when the EU is starting to implement its next strategy, The Agenda 2030 and its Sustainable Development Goals, covering the period 2021–2030 and when the academic and policy communities as well as the general public will be reflecting on the implementation of the previous one, Europe 2020. This book will be one of the first systematic contributions on the topic.

Part I. Setting up the strategic observatory for Europe 2030

2. The EU regional policy in the light of its past, present and future

To improve the economic well-being of regions in the European Union, the EU sets the regional policy also referred to as Cohesion Policy. It intends to avoid regional disparities by boosting regions, that are lacking behind.

Regional policy touches all parts of the EU, at all levels, from the EU-wide and national scale to Europe's regions and local communities (European Commission 2022k). The regional policy of the EU, or as the EU names it, the Cohesion Policy, aims to improve the economic well-being of regions in the EU and avoid regional disparities. It supports job creation, business competitiveness, economic growth, and sustainable development, and improves citizens' quality of life (European Commission 2022n). It acts as a redistributive mechanism for the European economy at large as well as a tool to leverage private capital in ways consistent with the EU's key strategy agendas with the ultimate aim of raising productivity and employment opportunities for all and 'ensuring Europe's global competitiveness (European Commission. Directorate General for Regional and Urban Policy, SWECO, and t33 2018). The policy is implemented by national and regional bodies in partnership with the European Commission (European Commission 2022k). This chapter aims to enlighten the changing policy throughout history and how it developed into the present. We will be considering its *variation*, how the priorities changed, how it is supported by the budget and which mechanisms are available for funding. Researching the current Cohesion Policy shows a quite complex approach not fully transparent to an ordinary EU citizen. While reading the EU Strategy, which sets six Commission priorities for 2019–2024, the regional aspect is not unambiguous. Namely, it is not the EU Strategy, that sets the regional development course but rather the regional development supports the EU Strategy selected indicators.

What is a region?

As is a case of determining any other terminology, defining regions and regional development is a thing of historic societal and economic evolution, viewed through the prism of different theoretical concepts. Further on, the definitions are followed by debates on adequate addressing the steering of the regional development by regional policies, how to disperse financial incentives and how to measure the impacts.

The European Union (EU) and its regional policy do not deviate from that notion. Starting with the basic question on "what is a region" stumbles not only into a theoretical conceptualization but also on how people live them. Coexistence and a feeling of belonging are two main driving forces, that shape municipalities and regions. If we look at the example of Slovenia, people identify themselves first by the village or town they live in and then by the municipality. Slovenians also tend to have a strong affiliation to their region, which coincides with the country's eleven statistical regions. The regional bonds tend to grow stronger when speaking about sports, the economy, and politics. However, the mentioned regions are not administrative units. There have been tendencies to enforce that kind of regime, but all efforts have been futile by now. One of the reasons might just lay in the fact, that those tendencies deflected the regional geography as people live and feel them for decades. By becoming an EU member state, Slovenia had to determine regions as understood by the EU NUTS 2. As Slovenia's territory is one of the smallest in Europe, the first attempts were to unite it as one region. From the point of being eligible for EU funding, that was not seen as acceptable, so two regions were enforced, one being more (the western) and one being less (the eastern) developed. It was a battle well played, but the division serves only competing for financial incentives and statistical comparison. These two newly established regions, as well as statistical ones, are not administrative units. The case of Slovenia is only one of the cases around the EU member states and the bottom-up image of the EU regions.

Regions are not progressing equally (Pandiloska Jurak 2021). Regions in the EU are also heavily diverse in size, population, and institutionalization. That being said, the NUTS 2 classification, which is used to disperse EU funds among regions is what the EU is operating with and as it is Sisyphus's work to rearrange it on the national level, it might be close to impossible to change on the EU level.

The policy formulation

The EU Cohesion Policy is a complex policy with a large budget, which is heavily influenced by membership changes and outside factors. To be able to understand the policy, one needs to know its' creation, namely how the process of the creation is set and who can participate in it.

From the programming and implementation point of view, the cohesion policy framework is established for 7 years. Implementation of the policy follows determined stages. First, the Commission prepares the proposal for the budget for the policy and the rules for its use which are then jointly decided by the European Council and the European Parliament. the Commission and the EU countries discuss the principles and priorities of cohesion policy through a process of consultation. Each Member State produces a draft Partnership Agreement prepared by each Member State, outlining the country's strategy and proposing a list of programmes. Cooperation programmes involving more than one country are also included. In the next stage, the Commission and the national authorities negotiate the final content of the Partnership Agreement, as well as each programme, which presents the priorities of the country and/or regions or the respected cooperation area. It is important to know, that in this stage, workers, employers and civil society bodies can all participate in the programming and management of the Ops (European Commission 2022l).

The implementation stage follows. It is carried out by the Member States and their regions implementing them. Due to selecting, monitoring, and evaluating hundreds of thousands of projects, the work is organised by managing authorities in each country and/or region. The moment when the Commission commits the funds, the countries are allowed to start spending on their programmes. The Commission also pays the certified expenditure to each country. The evaluation of the projects is also important, so the Commission monitors each programme, alongside the country concerned. In the last stage, both the Commission and the Member States submit reports throughout the programming period. (European Commission 2022l).

Even with the set system, the Cohesion Policy (see Crescenzi, Fratesi, and Monastiriotis 2020) can only deliver as a three-layered system (EU–member states–regions). If member states are punching below their weight, the entire architecture is weaker and less politically sustainable. The member states have heterogeneous preferences in terms of regional policy objectives and assessment of needs. Not all member states see internal regional disparities as a priority when compared with their 'aggregate' economic performance. They may favour efficiency over spatial equity, given their level of development as a whole country. Some countries have concentrated their resources on capital cities and their regions, other states give priority to investments in highly dense metropolitan areas in convergence regions. Countries have a different understanding and different operationalizations of the concept of territorial cohesion and shape their priorities according to their model of intervention. Due to that, national priorities and models of intervention should be made explicit by each member state so that the compatibility with higher-level EU-wide Cohesion objectives can be assessed explicitly (Crescenzi, Fratesi, and Monastiriotis 2020).

Cohesion policy historic development

The Cohesion policy historic development is a full display of the *variation, selection and retention* (concepts as understood by Jessop and Oosterlynck 2008) influenced by number of member states, economic and political circumstances. The regional policy was outlined in the Treaty of Rome founding the European Economic Community in 1957 (see Table 2 for a more systematic view of policies and data). In 1968 Directorate-General for Regional Policy of the European Commission was created, followed by the creation of the European Regional Development Fund in 1975 (European Commission 2022i). At that point, there were six member states (see Table 3). Leonardi (2006) says, that at that point the policy has been capable of concentrating considerable amounts of public and private investment in key areas of the economy (Leonardi 2006). Additionally, and what just might be one of the most important factors besides the financial stimulation, especially due to the ongoing membership expansions is Leonardi's findings, that the Cohesion policy represents more than a policy aimed at the spurring of economic development. Since 1989, cohesion has also taken on the vestiges of a political policy aimed at creating a more cohesive Union and a commitment to mutual solidarity between Europe's wealthier and poorer regions. (Leonardi 2006).

Table 2: The EU Cohesion policies in data

Time	Policy period	Designated funds in billion €	No. of member states	GDP per capita*	Population**
1957	1957–1987	n.d	6	n.d	n.d
1988	1988–1992	64	13	n.d	n.d
1995	1994–1999	168	15	18.940	373.125.330
2000	2000–2006	215	15	24.350	378.439.937
2004[1]	2000–2006	235	25	n.d.	460.554.941
2007	2007–2013	347	28	26.060	495.480.643
2014	2014–2021	351	28	27.750	508.178.973
2021	2021–2027	392	27	32.330	514.273.281

Source: Authors' display
* (European Commission 2022i)
** (Eurostat 2022)
*** (Worldbank 2022)
[1] the largest enlargement with 10 new member states was implemented

Table 3: The EU membership

	Countries		Number of EU Member states
1957 ("Founding fathers")	Belgium France Germany	Italy Luxembourg Netherlands	6
1973 (enlargement)	Denmark Ireland United Kingdom		9
1981 (enlargement)	Greece		10
1986 (enlargement)	Spain Portugal		12
1995 (enlargement)	Austria Finland Sweden		15
2004 (enlargement)	Czech Republic Estonia Cyprus Latvia Lithuania	Hungary Malta Poland Slovakia Slovenia	25
2007 (enlargement)	Romania Bulgaria		27
2013 (enlargement)	Croatia		28
2020 (ended membership)	United Kingdom		27

Source: *(European Commission 2022h)*, Authors own display

By 1988 adaptation of the policy was needed, due to the arrival of Greece (1981), Spain and Portugal (1986). The Structural Funds were integrated into an overarching cohesion policy, introducing key principles: focusing on the poorest and most backward regions, multi-annual programming strategic orientation of investments and involvement of regional and local partners. The designated budget was 64 billion EUR (European Commission 2022i). The reform of the Structural Funds gave the European Commission much greater influence on the distribution of regional development funding, in particular concerning the designation of eligible areas, the approval of Member State development plans, the management and delivery of programmes, and the control of expenditure (Bachtler and Wren 2006).

In 1993 the Maastricht Treaty introduced three novelties, two of them directly linked to the funding of the policy: the Cohesion Fund, the Committee of the

Regions, and the principle of subsidiarity. In the following years, two additional acts were implemented that had a direct impact on the policy: the Financial Instrument for Fisheries Guidance (created in 1993) and the resources for the structural and cohesion funds were doubled, to equal a third of the EU budget (1994–99). Additionally, a special objective was added to support the sparsely populated regions of Finland and Sweden in 1995. The budget from 1994 to 1999 was 168 billion (European Commission 2022i). The policy has favoured the convergence of less-developed regions towards the EU mean in terms of GDP per capita, rates of annual economic growth, employment levels and unemployment between 1988 and 1999, and thereafter (Leonardi 2006), with unemployment targeting young persons (Podmenik and Gorišek 2020).

The 'Lisbon Strategy' in 2000 shifted the EU's priorities toward growth, jobs, and innovation, which was also reflected in the priorities of the cohesion policy. Ten new countries joined the European Union in 2004, increasing the EU's population by 20 %, but its GDP by only 5 %. Due to the EU expansion, pre-accession instruments made funding and know-how available to countries waiting to join the EU in years from 2000 to 2004. From 200 to 2006, the budget amount was 213 billion for the 15 existing members and an additional 22 billion EUR for the new member countries (for the years 2004–06). The EU expanded again by welcoming Bulgaria and Romania in 2007 and Croatia in 2013. The Cohesion policy 2007 – 2013 implemented simplified rules and structures. It emphasised transparency and communication and an even stronger focus on growth and jobs are key elements of the reform. The budget was 347 billion EUR. 25 % of the budget has been earmarked for research and innovation, and 30 % for environmental infrastructure and measures to combat climate change (European Commission 2022i). In the analysis of the regional effects of EU Regional Policy during four programming periods 1989–1993, 1994–1999, 2000–2006, 2007–2013 Becker, Egger, and von Ehrlich (2018) find that adaptations regarding co-financing successfully strengthened the treatment effect of Objective 1 or Convergence Objective transfers on employment growth, however, the effect on income growth in particularly Crisis-prone regions was not convincing. Even more important from the point of view of shaping new policies is the conclusion that (Becker, Egger, and von Ehrlich 2018) transfers tend to display immediate effects, a t, period when it comes to stimulating real per-capita-income growth in recipient regions, they are not long-lived beyond programming. Once Objective 1 status is lost, previous growth gains seem to be disregarded. This finding supports the idea that Objective 1 should be kept for longer periods. Additionally, it should be geared towards investments that support long-term growth prospects. Otherwise, some regions might just see a one-off bonanza without any long-term benefits (Becker, Egger, and von Ehrlich 2018).

Research, done by Bachtrögler, Fratesi, and Perucca (2020) shows interesting results by comparing impact policy impact on the regions. They suggest that the impact of Cohesion Policy grants tends to be larger in relatively poor countries, such as Romania in CEE and Portugal among the EU-15 member states, where firms may face harder conditions and, maybe more in need of policy support. Local specificities of the region in which a beneficiary is located matter for the impact of Cohesion Policy firm grants on the supported firms' performance. In regions in which it is more difficult to gather private assets, firms are likely to be more in need of financial support than elsewhere to grow in employment, and value value-added productivity. On the one hand, in richer regions, a form of co-funding of the firm grant with the local budget could also make the policy impact stronger. Funding for regions or firms should be targeted in light of the units' particular characteristics and the expected impact at the same time (Bachtrögler, Fratesi, and Perucca 2020). Findings from Fiaschi, Lavezzi, and Parenti (2018) also point to a trade-off between the two goals of the EU Cohesion Policy of increasing overall growth and reducing inequalities. Especially Southern European regions are both the most peripheral and the poorest. If their economic backwardness and distance from the core of Europe would suggest to allocate them most of the funds to reduce inequalities, the decreasing marginal effect of Objective 1 funds on GDP per worker and their lower (positive) spatial externalities would suggest the opposite to increase overall growth (Fiaschi, Lavezzi, and Parenti 2018). Another point of view on the Cohesion Funds impact can be seen in the research, done by (Besednjak Valič, Kolar, and Lamut 2021). They argue, that due to the inhibitory functioning of state or national policies, the academia and business spheres are forced to seek support in EU projects (in their case for promoting the technology transfer) because, at the time, only EU funding through various projects can provide and deliver the necessary infrastructure and financial resources.

If in the past, the policy was not very straightforward in its objectives (in 2007 – 2013 they were named Objective 1, Objective 2 and Objective 3), the policy 2014 – 2021 was more transparent. The Europe 2020 Strategy was set for smart, sustainable, and inclusive growth in the European Union. It set a stronger focus on results with clearer and measurable targets for better accountability and was simplified by one set of rules for five Funds. Specific preconditions before funds can be channelled were introduced. The policy had an aim to strengthen the n urban dimension and fight for social inclusion: a minimum amount of ERDF earmarked for integrated projects in cities and ESF to support marginalised communities. The Commission enabled suspend funding for a Member State which does not comply with EU economic rules. Eleven thematic objectives of the Cohesion Policy were set to support the growth for the period 2014–2020. The budget amount of 351 billion EUR was to be drawn from investments from the ERDF which would support all 11 objectives, but 1–4 are the main priorities for investment, European Social Fund with main priorities 8–11 and the Cohesion Fund to support objectives 4–7 and 11 (European Commission 2022j). Since the financial framework and the implementation of all approved projects have finished, the evaluation of the policy is not possible yet. What one can observe is, that the experts and the Commission will have to think about the long-term effect of its policies. For instance: is "green" electricity de facto so "green"? Is its production green as well? What happens to the infrastructure when it meets its expiration date? There are already issues with expired wind power plants.

What lays ahead

Researching the current Cohesion Policy shows a quite complex approach not fully transparent to an ordinary EU citizen. While reading the EU Strategy, which sets six Commission priorities for 2019–2024, the regional aspect is not unambiguous. Namely, it is not the EU Strategy, that sets the regional development course but rather the regional development supports the EU Strategy selected indicators.

In 2021–2027 EU cohesion policy has set a shorter list of 5 policy objectives supporting growth for the period 2021–2027: (1) a more competitive and smarter Europe, (2) a greener, low-carbon transitioning toward a net zero carbon economy. (3) a more connected Europe by enhancing mobility (4) a more social and inclusive Europe and (5) Europe closer to citizens by fostering the sustainable and integrated development of all types of territories. In addition to that, the policy sets climate targets as weighted climate and environmental contribution of investments, minimum targets for funds, and climate adjustment mechanism. The new policy aims to achieve greater empowerment of local, urban & territorial authorities in the management of the funds by dedicating policy objectives implemented only through territorial and local development strategies It also tends to be more flexible as in flexible programming adjusted to new challenges and emerging needs (European Commission 2022k).

Yet again, it is not only the need of steering the development as such but rather a broader impact, that needs to be met by this policy. As Crescenzi, Fratesi, and Monastiriotis (2020) argue, the recent European Elections in May 2019 have made apparent the urgency of balancing in the most effective manner conflicting instances encompassing issues such as the political handling of populist movements and, consequently, the management of the EU's external and internal borders that all have strong regional connotations and patterns. In this context of tense political confrontation on its goals and intervention logic as well as highly regionally asymmetric (social, political, and demographic) challenges, the Cohesion Policy is requested to be impactful and effective. It is asked to deliver on wider objectives of modernizing the European economic space and dealing effectively with new social risks and not only on the objective of social, economic and territorial cohesion (Crescenzi, Fratesi, and Monastiriotis 2020). In 2020, when the mentioned chapter was published, also other crises emerged in a form of Covid 19, the war between Ukraine and Russia (which by itself shook Europe with price speculation, speculation in gas and oil deficit etc.) and environmental changes, that we can no longer ignore. If the policy and stakeholders will deliver remains to be seen.

The priorities of the 2021–2027 policy were set also on the level of funds for 392 billion EUR: the European Regional Development Fund supported investments of all 5 policy objectives, but 1 and 2 are the main priorities, the European Social Fund+ main priority is 4, the Cohesion Fund supports policy objectives 2 and 3, the Just Transition Fund provides support under dedicated specific objectives, The Interreg programmes have 2 additional policy objectives at their disposal: "A better cooperation governance" and "A safer and more secure Europe". To support simplified fund withdrawal, the new cohesion policy introduces one set single of rules for the eight Funds and a significant reduction in the amount of secondary legislation. This entails notably: lighter and more frequent reporting; lighter controls for programmes in a form of sharp reduction of management verifications, "single audit principle", proportionate arrangements for audits; faster delivery in a form of extended possibility to use simplified cost options (SCOs) and financing not linked to costs schemes; end of Commission approval for major projects and no more designation of management and control bodies (European Commission 2022e). Regarding the eligibility of regions, changes were made in a way, that some regions just might not meet the criteria anymore. The stipulations on what is a "more developed", "transition" and "less developed" region diverse from 2014–2022 to 2021–2027 policy. The co-financing has changed as well (see Table 4).

Governance, impact, and evaluation

At times of tighter budgets, voters and politicians in net contributing countries and regions ask about the justification of such EU budget dedicated funds, even

Table 4: EU region development level

	2014–2020	*2021–2027*
Less developed regions	GDP per capita < 75 % EU-27 average **Co-financing:** 80 % or 85 % (crisis impact)	GDP per capita < 75 % EU-27 average **Co-financing:** 85 %
Transition regions	GDP per capita between 75 % and 90 % EU-27 average **Co-financing:** 60 % or 80 % (ex LDR)	GDP per capita between 75 % and 100 % EU-27 average **Co-financing:** 60 % or 70 % (ex LDR)
More developed regions	GDP per capita > 90 % EU-27 average **Co-financing:** 50 %	GDP per capita > 100 % EU-27 average **Co-financing:** 40 % or 50 % (would have been TRR under 2014–20 period)

Source: (European Commission 2022e), Authors own display

more so than at times of economic prosperity (Becker, Egger, and von Ehrlich 2018). The combination of large amounts of expenditure and argued decisions on its usage have led to pressure for more accountability in spending, which is reflected in the creation of a steadily more extensive EU evaluation regime, as well as more binding obligations for the monitoring, financial management and auditing of expenditure (Bachtler and Wren 2006). We have already mentioned a few studies on the implementation and evaluation of the policy impacts. We will not devote more time to going deeper into this subject but would rather outline the obstacles when evaluating such a complex policy.

A large strand of the literature suggests that there is a lack of consistency among studies which may be caused by two kinds of heterogeneity characterizing the Cohesion Policy. First, the Cohesion Policy may finance a broad variety of actions, some more focused on the economic return of investments, others on the achievement of progress in the social sphere. Second, the Cohesion Policy is implemented in highly diversified territorial settings that may affect the outcome of the communitarian action ({Citation}). The complexity also arises from the nature of the policy being evaluated. Structural and Cohesion Funds programmes are implemented under a common regulatory framework, but in widely differing national and regional circumstances with varied institutional arrangements for managing and delivering regional development policy (Bachtler and Wren 2006). EU-wide aggregated results might hide important differences and mask significant country-level heterogeneity and composition effects. The question is are regional economic impacts persistently diversified across countries? (Crescenzi and Giua 2020).

Further on, programmes comprise a range of interventions, through a mix of financial instruments and many different types of beneficiaries. Also, EU support has to be co-financed with national public or private funding that may originate in several different organizations or schemes (Bachtler and Wren 2006). Blom-Hansen (2005) suggest that when evaluated through the lens of the principal-agent framework, it becomes apparent that EU control mechanisms are weak. As agents, the member states are likely to have national concerns closer at heart than goals formulated at the EU level, and the implementation contract between the EU and the member states does not provide the member states with any incentives to stay loyal to EU goals. EU monitoring of the member state implementation measures seems effective, but implementation deficits are difficult to sanction owing to policy conflicts among the multiple EU principals (Blom-Hansen 2005). Crescenzi, Fratesi, and Monastiriotis (2020) also note that the role, preferences and involvement of individual member states have regained a strong momentum. On the other hand, if we look at the existing scholarly and policy literature on Cohesion Policy, the debate has largely focused on the two institutional and spatial end-points (either the EU 'centre' or the 'regions') with limited attention to the national level. Narrow attention has been placed at the national level not only as the intermediate level connecting the two endpoints but also as the key institutional and economic intermediary and the main hot spot of political strain. The unitary and homogenous nature of the policy across member states is given as granted by research on Cohesion Policy that adopts an EU-wide top-down perspective, often overlooking the developmental or political preconditions, inclinations and constraints of the individual member states. Other approaches have adopted a regional bottom-up perspective, assuming that the bulk of the policy leadership should come from individual regions, but also overlooking the role of the national level in shaping capacities and external and internal constraints (Crescenzi, Fratesi, and Monastiriotis 2020).

The EU Cohesion policy is different in both its structure and impact from national regional policies, and this is particularly evident in its emphasis on the multilevel government approach to the implementation of the policy. Multi lever governance has allowed the entry into the policy process of several actors (subnational governments and socio-economic partners) that before had often been systematically excluded from any role in national regional policy, and a renewed emphasis on the importance of institution-building and administrative capacity as components in the determination of positive policy outputs and outcomes (Leonardi 2006). When investigating the national link in the long principal–agent chain involved in the implementation of EU cohesion policy, the multi-level governance literature's investigations of national policy networks, specifications of participating actors, differences between unitary and federal member states, and mappings of formal and informal rules and resource asymmetries would be well worth taking into account (Blom-Hansen 2005).

The most recent studies on the impacts of Cohesion Policy have approached the definition of a suitable counterfactual scenario by adopting treatment effect methods. Policy impacts, such as terms of economic growth and employment, are netted out from the confounding influence of all other characteristics of the territorial ecosystem in which the policy effect is embedded (Crescenzi and Giua 2020).

Different possibilities of evaluation bring different results. This means, that they can be exploited in one's interests. As Bachtler and Wren (2006) say, valuation serves the objective of many different organizations, such as programme managers, partners with regional and national government authorities, various European institutions and so on. Each has its motives and interests in the results and implementation of the EU spending (Bachtler and Wren 2006). It is necessary to pay special attention to the selection of a model, examine the potential results and find possible solutions to correct deficiencies (Pandiloska Jurak and Pinteric 2012). Furthermore, consistency and transparency are not needed only throughout the different policies and strategic goals but also throughout their retention to assure the set goal (Pandiloska Jurak 2019). There could be an interesting (different) approach to measuring of regional achievements.

The Organization for Economic Cooperation and Development (OECD) work on regional development covers several interrelated fields, namely statistics and indicators, regional innovation (on innovation indicators see also (Erman 2020)), multi-level governance and public finance, water governance, urban and metropolitan policy and rural development. OECD started asking on-point questions, which we could say are set from the "bottom-up" point of view: Are our lives getting better? How can policies improve our lives? Are we measuring the right things? The OECD Better Life Initiative and the work programme on Measuring Well-Being and Progress answer these questions. They allow understanding of what drives the well-being of people and nations and what needs to be done to achieve greater progress for all. (see OECD 2022a). OECD has concluded that past policies have failed to reduce regional disparities significantly and have not been able to help individual lagging regions to catch up, despite the allocation of significant public funding. The result is the under-used economic potential and weakened social cohesion (OECD 2022b). OECD claims, that work on regional development recognises a new approach to regional development is emerging; one that promises more effective use of public resources and significantly better policy outcomes. It involves a shift away from redistribution and subsidies for lagging regions in favour of measures to increase the competitiveness of all regions (ibid). In 2011, a list of 11 topics of well-being was published. Each of the 11 topics is made up of 1–4 indices and these are fine-tuned over time as insights are derived from data collected in previous years: housing (housing conditions and spending), income (household income and net financial wealth), jobs (earnings, job security and unemployment), community (quality of social support network), education (education and what one gets out of it), environment (quality of environment), governance (involvement in a democracy), health, life satisfaction (level of happiness), safety (murder and assault rates) and work-life balance (OECD 2022b). Namely, it does not focus solely on the GDP. The GDP measures the added value, created through the production of goods and services, which indirectly tells the story of a society, that is well educated, which indirectly indicates having funds (state or personal) to be able to finance it. However, there is a statistic behind that, which just might hide big disparities among very well and very low-paid workers and it does not show more complex insight into the societal day-to-day life. In other words, the OECD approach turns the focus from economic benefits to societal benefits.

The Better Life Index is designed to let you visualise and compare some of the key factors, such as education, housing, and environment, that contribute to well-being in OECD countries. It is being visualised through an interactive tool that allows you to see how countries perform according to the importance *one gives* to each of the 11 topics that make for a better life (ibidem.).

3. Discourses swirling the implementation of the grand strategies: Case of New Industrial Strategy

In past years the global trends have been shifting and shaping due to globalisation, increased individualisation and consumer demands (Singh et al. 2009). Following the consumer demands, the consumer preferences also shifted towards sustainability, and so-called eco-isms. The drivers behind it are definitely the increased availability of knowledge, especially related to climate change and ecological topics. The past year shifts and events happening surrounding the Covid-19 outbreak and war in Ukraine emphasises the needs to turn inwards for consumers even more. Within this conundrum the traditionally aside looking industrial aspects is emerging to the forefront of the discussions.

Namely, it was Ursula von der Leyen who mentioned, at the start of her turn, and immediately before the Covid-19 outbreak, the need for a strong European Industrial Policy. The New Industrial Strategy that will foster innovation and development, and while doing this also ensure jobs (Alcidi et al. 2021). The new industrial policy that will satisfy the needs to be environmentally friendly and sustainable, and will foster new approached, from open innovation to technology transfer and circularity. As such it is in line with Europe 2030 agenda. But, having said all of the above, how should the countries and the EU approach such new industrial policy? Traditionally, in the minds of the people, the industry, related inevitably with manufacturing is associated with something dirty and environment polluting. At this stage, the European Industry will no longer able to be manufacturing per se (Aiginger and Rodrik 2020) but will have to be future and welfare oriented. However, to achieve this goal, politicians steering the process will have to develop and implement proper policies for the success of such ambitious goals. Aiginger and Rodrik (2020) admit, the government has to steer such process while relying to the information from industry sector and being at the same time aware such information might be biased. Based on this we define out main research question of this discussion: In what ways it is possible to steer the discourses surrounding the creation and implementation of New Industrial Policy in the EU? With posing this question we admit the need to establish a proper discourse of semiotic usage of language to create a joint imaginary for people to identify with it and therefore follow it easier. Approach in establishing theoretic economic imaginaries is put forward by Jessop and Oosterlynck (Jessop and Oosterlynck 2008).

Industry; a yes or a no?

Continuing the argument from above – traditionally the industry was associated with heavy machinery, dirty manufacturing and negative impacts to the immediate and wider local environment (Besednjak Valič 2019). It was the 1970s when the heavy and dirty industries started to move offshore – seeking cheaper labour force in the newly opening far east economies. EU was not an exception to this trend. Different global forces and geopolitical dynamics contributed to the fact that developed EU countries adopted the same approach of such industrial migration also to the countries of the immediate EU borders. These countries have become the member states in the last 20 years as the EU expanded and their industrial policies and subsequent question of policy adoption become relevant also for them. Following the argument adopting Sum and Jessop stance on re-imaginations (Sum and Jessop 2013), this is the dynamic we detect within the Industrial policy and its change in the past years. The reason for the change was partially the economic crisis, as initiated in 2008, and as the authors claim, the crisis is always a good extra-semiotic (Sum and Jessop 2013) cause to influence the retention of the imaginary (Sum and Jessop 2013; Jessop and Oosterlynck 2008).

However, to get a better insight of the economic development the European countries reached, an interesting calculation is available below in Table 5. It is in the Table 5 we can observe the average GDP of period 2012–2021 for each of the countries. In columns two and three the percentual increase is monitored in relation to both bordering dates. In numerous countries, especially those who joined the EU in 2004 this progress is even more noticeable. Countries like Czech Republic, Estonia and Slovenia seem as success stories, and similarly other who joined the EU after 2007 (Croatia, Bulgaria, and Romania) with the notion, the average GDP remains way below the EU average.

In periods of transitioning from industrial stage to service providing stage, many countries decided to de-industrialise, among two predominant cases are Spain and Greece, but also several regions within and outside the EU followed the same path. But the data from Table 5 demonstrate it is Greece and Spain, who are not progressing in terms of GDP per capita. At the first glance it is noticeable the strong orientation towards service sector, traditionally tourism, does not contribute towards increase in GPR per capita. In elaboration of the argument, the Table 6 elaborated the shares of industry in GDP. It is seen the Spain and

Table 5: GDP per capita as indicator of development

	Average GDP 2012–2021	Year 2012 with respect to average	Year 2021 with respect to average
European Union – 27 countries (from 2020)	28.716,00 €	-10,3 %	12,4 %
Belgium	38.520,00 €	-9,7 %	13,6 %
Bulgaria	7.368,00 €	-21,6 %	33,7 %
Czechia	18.027,00 €	-14,2 %	23,8 %
Denmark	50.383,00 €	-9,6 %	13,8 %
Germany	38.562,00 €	-11,5 %	11,3 %
Estonia	17.719,00 €	-23,7 %	30,1 %
Ireland	59.188,00 €	-35,5 %	41,9 %
Greece	16.507,00 €	3,4 %	3,8 %
Spain	23.966,00 €	-8,0 %	6,2 %
France	33.860,00 €	-6,0 %	7,9 %
Croatia	11.900,00 €	-12,4 %	23,6 %
Italy	28.292,00 €	-4,6 %	6,2 %
Cyprus	23.191,00 €	-3,0 %	12,2 %
Latvia	13.742,00 €	-20,9 %	27,0 %
Lithuania	14.809,00 €	-24,5 %	33,4 %
Luxembourg	97.526,00 €	-10,2 %	17,3 %
Hungary	12.635,00 €	-20,0 %	25,6 %
Malta	23.517,00 €	-25,5 %	18,8 %
Netherlands	43.026,00 €	-9,4 %	14,1 %
Austria	41.380,00 €	-8,6 %	8,8 %
Poland	12.100,00 €	-16,8 %	24,4 %
Portugal	18.413,00 €	-13,1 %	11,5 %
Romania	9.356,00 €	-29,2 %	33,7 %
Slovenia	20.512,00 €	-14,1 %	20,3 %
Slovakia	15.485,00 €	-12,4 %	15,1 %
Finland	40.622,00 €	-8,6 %	12,3 %

(Continued)

Table 5: Continued

	Average GDP 2012–2021	Year 2012 with respect to average	Year 2021 with respect to average
Sweden	46.715,00 €	-3,3 %	9,0 %
Iceland	51.630,00 €	-30,7 %	12,4 %
Norway	69.908,00 €	13,0 %	7,8 %
Switzerland	73.129,00 €	-7,9 %	7,9 %

Source: (EUROSTAT 2022b), own calculation

Table 6: Shares of GDP in industry among selected European countries

	Average 2001–2010	Average 2011–2021	Difference
European Union – 27 countries (from 2020)	18,7	17,9	-0,8
European Union – 28 countries (2013–2020)	18,1	17,2	-0,9
Belgium	17,8	15,0	-2,7
Bulgaria	18,9	19,5	0,5
Czechia	27,6	27,4	-0,2
Denmark	17,3	15,9	-1,5
Germany	22,7	22,7	-0,1
Estonia	18,9	18,3	-0,6
Ireland	23,2	30,8	7,6
Greece	11,9	12,4	0,5
Spain	16,4	14,8	-1,6
France	14,4	12,4	-2,0
Croatia	17,6	16,6	-1,0
Italy	18,1	17,3	-0,9
Cyprus	8,6	6,8	-1,7
Latvia	14,8	14,1	-0,7
Lithuania	21,0	20,2	-0,8
Luxembourg	8,9	6,1	-2,8
Hungary	22,0	21,4	-0,6

Table 6: Continued

	Average 2001–2010	Average 2011–2021	Difference
Malta	15,4	9,7	-5,7
Netherlands	16,0	14,2	-1,8
Austria	20,9	19,6	-1,2
Poland	21,5	22,3	0,8
Portugal	15,6	15,2	-0,4
Romania	26,1	24,2	-1,9
Slovenia	23,6	23,3	-0,3
Slovakia	24,9	22,6	-2,4
Finland	23,6	17,9	-5,7
Sweden	20,3	16,6	-3,7
Iceland	14,5	14,8	0,3
Norway	31,7	26,7	-5,0
Switzerland	21,1	20,0	-1,0

Source: (EUROSTAT 2022c), own calculation

Greece exhibit the among the lowest levels of GDP in industry in the EU. The shares are ranging between 11,9 % – 12,4 % (smallest of increases) for Spain, and 16,4 % – 14,8 % (small decrease). On the other hand, the most successful EU countries in terms of percentages are Ireland, Poland, Czech Republic, Bulgaria, but also Slovenia and Slovakia. Among the mentioned Ireland, Poland, and Bulgaria monitor slight increase in industry shares in GDP, with the rest monitoring either same or slight decrease. In the last two decades, for majority of EU countries the shares of industry in GDP are rather stable, with small decreases over the years. However, Heymann and Vetter (2013) conclude, about countries of traditional EU core stagnating while the countries of Eastern EU flourish, both in terms of shares of industrial sector in GDP as well as added value of the industry.

It is additionally noted that countries with certain level of strong industrial policy are dominating the scale for the EU in terms of GDP per capita. The countries who have not shifted to full-service sector and were able to obtain own industrial capacity are currently looking very prosperous in this perspective. We are here again referring to Germany, Greece, and Spain as the main examples of the outlined argument. However, as according to Heymann and Vetter (2013), since 2000 the overall gross share of industry in GDP has decreased for numerous EU countries on the expense of increasing share of services, the authors also outline the problem of deteriorating international competitiveness of those countries. It was the industrialised countries like Germany and Scandinavian countries that were able to maintain competitiveness but the other countries have fallen behind.

Namely, the industrial sector is the sector that that has significant impact on labour market. Even if one takes into account the demographic changes, the industrial and ICT development of new technologies the demographic change is inevitable and national ecosystems are starting to compete to attract skilled labour force. As noted from the Eurostat data on shares of employment in industry across Europe, the data (see below Table 7) demonstrates the countries of the Danube region to obtain the highest shares of persons employed in industry. And this is even along the fact these same countries are facing large demographic changes in terms of brain drain, aging of population and concentration of population in cities where the industries are traditionally not as present. An interesting additional insight is offered by the data of the shares of GDP industry contributes. The Table 6 reveals that in some countries, like Germany, Norway, and Switzerland where the industry occupies large proportions of GDP (consult Table 6) and it does so, even despite employing lower shares of persons. These dynamics only shows the potential in added value of digitalisation and innovation occurring in industrial sectors.

Table 7: Employed in industry; percentage of total employed

	Average 2001–2010	*Average 2011–2021*	*Difference*
European Union – 28 countries (2013–2020)	17,4	15,4	-2,0
Belgium	15,0	12,1	-3,0
Bulgaria	22,2	20,0	-2,2
Czechia	29,5	28,7	-0,8
Denmark	13,6	10,9	-2,7
Germany (until 1990 former territory of the FRG)	19,9	18,6	-1,3
Estonia	24,0	21,2	-2,7
Ireland	15,1	11,4	-3,6

Table 7: Continued

	Average 2001–2010	Average 2011–2021	Difference
Greece	11,5	9,3	-2,2
Spain	14,9	11,3	-3,6
France	12,9	10,6	-2,3
Croatia	22,0	20,3	-1,7
Italy	19,6	17,1	-2,5
Cyprus	11,2	9,5	-1,8
Latvia	18,0	16,2	-1,9
Lithuania	19,4	17,9	-1,5
Luxembourg	12,1	8,9	-3,2
Hungary	24,9	21,0	-3,9
Malta	19,8	12,3	-7,5
Netherlands	10,8	9,3	-1,5
Austria	17,5	16,0	-1,5
Poland	23,3	23,3	0,0
Portugal	18,6	16,7	-1,9
Romania	23,3	21,3	-2,0
Slovenia	26,4	22,8	-3,5
Slovakia	26,4	23,8	-2,5
Finland	18,2	14,7	-3,5
Sweden	16,4	13,0	-3,3
Iceland	13,4	13,0	-0,4
Norway	13,1	11,6	-1,4
Switzerland	16,3	14,4	-1,8

Source: (EUROSTAT 2022a), own calculation

Industry – the back bone of the EU and the question of re-industrialisation

In the years, following the economic crisis that started in 2012 it become evident that unregulated free-market capitalism has its deficiencies (Bartlett 2014). Deindustrialisation we oftentimes accompanied by the rise of the financial sector, and as such the countries were left vulnerable to destructive financial bubbles (see also Bartlett 2014).The crisis has provided a loss of confidence to the suggestions of neo-liberal economic theories that prescribed the sole reliance on market rules (Bartlett 2014). It was the given situation where the question of re-industrialisation of Europe become relevant. Apart from this, another set of factors become important: rising power of China, on the one hand, but also the need for employment in home countries and question of obtaining the power over knowledge. The industrial sector has always been (Camarinha-Matos et al. 2019) interrelated to innovation and knowledge, it become inevitable – the need to protect the knowledge and also the know-how for domestic purposes. The countries of the EU have started to recognise this vial intertwinement between knowledge and industry, they have decided, that industry needs to be brought back to the EU. The condition being the environmental consideration, the upgrades and innovative performance. The question of re-industrialisation is therefore the question or re-imagination (Sum and Jessop 2013). The difference with the approach outlined by Jessop and co-workers is only in the nature of the semiotic causes for the change. So far the crisis (Sum and Jessop 2013) was outlined as the most evident extra-semiotic cause for the change in the imaginary, and one can pose a question whether the current situations in the EU and the world are not just the right ones for the another change of the imaginary?

Not to deviate from the main argument, the focus on the industrialisation, or even re-industrialisation was recognised in several countries and they adopted different approaches, with one common denominator. The strong role of the government and its supporting agencies and services to monitor the success – of both, the industrial sector and measures set by the policy (Aiginger and Rodrik 2020). Additionally, Heymann and Vetter (2013) claim that contemporary views over industry are fairly positive – they even compare the attitudes to a renaissance. We can agree that one of the main reasons can be the current economic success of Germany, as strongest EU industrial country. It was Germany who was most successful dealing with the past economic crisis (Besednjak Valič 2019) and still is Germany as one among the most successful post-Covid 19 countries based on OECD evaluations (OECD 2021). Apart from this, the notable fall in shares of the manufacturing in GDP is decreasing in recent years. Heymann and Vetter (2013) report this decline for all the countries except for Germany. However, it is the aim of the EU to have the share of manufacturing in GDP set at 20 % by 2020. As this goal did not come true for several countries and even for the EU average, there are countries who are exceeding it. Countries like Germany and Scandinavian countries, are experiencing fastest growth and development. However, it is not with standing the fact, the mentioned countries are reaching yet to reach the status of most developed or developmental leader. Can we say, the investment in industry and the knowledge related to it proves to be the path towards not only economic but also societal?

Apart from the economic success of the industrial countries in recent years, also the new narratives related to industry and industrial development have been emerging and gaining momentum (Camarinha-Matos et al. 2019). The industry and manufacturing is not considered related to pollution, environmental hazards and overall "smoking chimneys" but the societal narrative goes in a direction towards expressing its relation to knowledge society, digitalisation, the 4th industrial revolution and everything related to the 'Industry 4.0' concept (Camarinha-Matos et al. 2019), oftentimes named as 'Industry 4.0' in Germany, or 'Smart Manufacturing' in USA (ibid.). In the same manner, the EU launched the 'Factories of the Future' programme. This transition was driven by advancements of ICT focusing at convergence of physical and virtual worlds (Camarinha-Matos et al. 2019). Other names include also the 'cyber-physical System' (CPS) and the idea was gradually adopted in industry as 'cyber-physical production System' (CPPS) (ibid.). Soon idea developed in to combination of CPS, 'Internet of Things' (IoT) and 'Internet of Services' (IoS). The perspective was supported by terms like 'smartness', 'smart machines', 'smart sensors', 'smart factory', 'smart environments', 'smart products' etc. (ibid.). What become notable it was not that industry become related to innovation, technology transfer and overall highly skilled labour force (Besednjak Valič 2019; Pandiloska Jurak 2020), but it related industry to subfields like: engineering, computer science and artificial intelligence, intertwined in manufacturing.

To sum up, the processes gained momentum (Camarinha-Matos et al. 2019) where support for industrial transformation and even re-industrialization and revitalization opened the space for stakeholders to discuss the new industrial directions. Lastly, this turn is noticeable also in the bulk of scientific literature written on the subject matter. All of the above supports the claim of successful re-imagination (as defined by Sum and Jessop 2013) when it comes to industrial strategy and the vision of industry in EU imaginary.

European approaches towards industrial policies in search for their efficiency

The EU as a post WWII project placed a bet on strong industry sectors following the Fordist production: steel, automotive, and chemicals (Pianta 2014; Hafner and Modic 2020), and in the 1070s the new fields emerged: aircraft, electronics, and biotechnology. A lot of different types of incentives were offered to encourage the development of the before mentioned sectors, along with the mechanism of the state-owned-enterprises (ibid.). It is France, that Pianta (2014) cites as the most vivid example of the transformation of the attitudes towards industrial policy: In post WWII France, the main actors of the industrial policy were the Ministries, sectoral agencies, and state owned enterprises, oftentimes managed by the elite National Schools graduates (ibid. p. 280). However, the neoliberal approaches emerging in the 1980s initiated the doubts towards such approaches. The large state-owned enterprises were privatised, as the discourse turned towards assuring the markets are able to operate efficiently in both short and long term. The privatisations led to extensive closing downs, foreign takeovers and greater market concentrations (ibid.). Following this line of thought, the space for the industrial policies was at this stage diminished and reduced, and no integrated industrial policy was at the forefront of the EU. Following this, the national industrial policies were only able to follow the paths of medium turn incentives and building of horizontal mechanisms. As Pianta (2014) concludes, what followed was a general loss of policy influence on the industrial change and development throughout Europe and in many countries this meant a great loss of industrial activities (ibid. p. 280) and also causing premature de-industrialisation (Aiginger and Rodrik 2020). As elaborated above, premature de-industrialisation can cause problem in desires for re-industrialisation, as the knowledge base and labour force skills are transferred to other sectors. Similar situation can be noted at places, where declining industrialisation was vastly replaced by gambling and similar service industries. The most vivid examples are here city of Nova Gorica, Slovenia and Atlantic City in USA (Besednjak Valič, 2014).

It is not so recent the questions of efficient industry policy came to the forefront of the researchers. Several authors have provided re-statements in this regard. See for example Chang (1994), Hausmann and Rodrik (2003), Rodrik (2008), Wade (2012), and Greenwald and Stiglitz (2013). Their argument went to the direction where it is not the industry that is questionable, but rather the ways in which such policy is to be carried out. Without a doubt, such debates result to have more value for contrived more depending on the industry as in the knowledge society, the industry is no longer associated with smoking chimneys but rather to knowledge, innovation, technology transfer and digital transformation (Besednjak Valič 2019). Similarly, several research explore on how new industrialised countries invest efforts in developing extensive public policies, combining public and private efforts to develop knowledge and get involved in other technology transfer related processes. For further reading see also Cimoli, Dosi, and Stiglitz (2009), and Stiglitz and Yifu (2013). In this context, especially interesting are the cases of Asia and Korea (Lee 2013a; 2013b; Freire 2013).

Having said all this, we are currently well entering the 2030 perspectives (2030 Agenda) that are far more ambitious than the Lisbon treaty and Europe 2020 were. It was the Lisbon treaty that set the ambitious goals to transition to knowledge society, emphasising the scientific research, technology, development of trade, and internal market among other goals (Lucian 2015). The problem of the Lisbon treaty is noted as targeting the area that were out of scope of areas of European economic integration. This is seen as the reason the majority of EU countries proved to be severely underperforming at mid-term evaluation of the strategy (ibid.). It was the period after 2010 that new set of challenges was detected – the economic crisis caused millions of layoffs and European members of parliament called for "Europeans need millions of jobs" (Lucian 2015, p. 58). After the failure of Lisbon treaty (Rončević 2019; Makarovič, Šušteršič, and Rončević 2014; Haverland and Romeijn 2007), the Europe 2020 was adopted demanding of national member states to closely monitor and report the goals set by it.

Making sure the New Industrial Strategy 2030 works

The interesting situation occurs if we put ourselves in a position trying to understand what happened in the year prior to 2020. If one aims in understanding of the dynamics from the evolutionary point of view, we can fully agree with the conclusions of Makarovič et al. (Makarovič, Šušteršič, and Rončević 2014) and Rončević (Rončević 2019) on the importance of steering the discourses surrounding the policy implementation. It is up to the policy makers to be able to transfer the policy into so called imaginary (Jessop and Oosterlynck 2008). The imaginary is a defined as joint narrative all the actors in the system agree to and work towards its implementation(Jessop and Oosterlynck 2008). The intriguing question arises if we start examining the path towards implementation of the New Industrial Strategy as evolutionary mechanism on the run. Through the variation, selection, and retention phases, we can conclude the narrative towards the importance of the industry changed in the past years. The change goes mainly on behalf of public statements and policy mix proposed to support the knowledge, technology, innovation and digitalisation-based industry that will contribute towards jobs, constructing another imaginary – the one of sustainable growth.

As we were able to observe, some steps were already made in this direction by the shift of narrative supporting the industry as main job creation sector (Lucian

2015). But the main question in this context remains – are the efforts sufficient and is the narrative going to support the implementation of the strategy? Based on writings of prominent researchers, the contemporary western society is in constant flux and the flux can be steered by selection and retention of the chosen narrative. The narrative can transform into economic imaginary (Jessop and Oosterlynck 2008) write, however when applying the concept to policy implementation a strict operationalisation is required. Namely, grand strategies, determined to form new economic imaginary inevitably need the vastest support possible, as (Mazzucato, Kattel, and Ryan-Collins 2020) place it: Challenges are necessarily cross-sectoral; they require stimulating demand and expectations of firms and investors. We add – and consumers. In order to be able to be sure the narrative is going to be successful; the stakeholders' needs to be steered in direction to adopt the set goals as their own.

Having said all that we can sum up, the industrial policies for the 21st century should promote the narratives (Aiginger and Rodrik 2020) of manufacturing as crucial for growth and wellbeing; industrial policy as systemic and based on capabilities, ambitions, and preferences. Industrial policy should take the high road and redirect the technical progress, be prepared for less growth, and focused on societal goals. In this regards, the authors propose the industrial policy to be a systemic approach coordinating innovation, regional and trade policies along with manufacturing at its core (Aiginger and Rodrik 2020). By promoting selected narratives, the processes of selection are already put in place and contribute towards retention of the selected discourse. This way the imaginary is established (Sum and Jessop 2013). Doing so, the policy desired to successfully implements the developmental strategy will succeed.

The EU communicates, it is the new Industrial Strategy that has laid foundations for an industrial policy that will support twin transitions, and make EU more competitive globally. At the same time, it desires to enhance Europe's strategic autonomy (COM 2021). The latest Industry strategy therefore outlines the fact the EU was always the home of the industry (COM 2020). The common vision is therefore, the desire for the industrial strategy to reflect the values and social market traditions. The strategy aims to comply with the highest social, labour and environmental standards, to promote opportunities in localisation, support sustainability and social rights. The industrial strategy was set with the purpose to also support world leading industry while pave the way to climate neutrality and shaping digital future. This will be reached by stronger digital single market, circular economy and promoted industrial innovation. the skilled and reskilled workforce and financing of transition will be the tasks to tackle while the EU industrial and strategic autonomy will be reinforced. The partnership approach to governance will additionally serve to strengthen the goals and strategic alliances and partnerships will be encouraged.

Based on all said and based on the complexity and diversity of the adopted goals the main question persists: how to steer the discourse to be able to achieve the desired result: the joint imaginary where the industrial strategy is seen as one grand strategy where all jointly contribute to make it happen? Partially a response is offered by communication strategists who would advise on key topics for key audiences at key moment through key communication tools. But the creation of imaginary is much more than just communication. It is a joint belief, as the prosperous and connected Europe was immediately after the WW2.

In order to overcome its traditional democratic deficit, all stakeholders will have to be mobilised in order to support the narrative of the selected discourse. The new industrial strategy is ambitions and its goals are very wide in nature. In this regard, not only triple helix stakeholders will suffice, but the civil society as well. So, in order to be able to steer the dominating discourse the EU will have use all tools including education system to promote the long-term strategic goals. As example, support the reorganisation of schools' curricula to support knowledge society, nurture innovation and foster cooperation.

4. How consistent is the EU policy? From formulation to assessment and evaluation. The case of research and innovation

From the European Coal and Steel Community in 1951, many treaties added new layers of sophistication, creating what we know today as the European Union (EU). With the treaty of Rome, some clear concepts of Economic and Energy cooperation are established, setting up the pillars of the EU. As the timeline progressed, the established community grew, not only advancing in coordination (e.g., Brussels Treaty in 1965; and lately the treaty of Lisbon in 2009) but also in number (starting with Denmark, Ireland and the United Kingdom in 1973, and lastly with Croatia in 2013) (European Union 2022a). With all that, the European Union is a unique concept. It is not an international alliance in common sense. The degree of integration, the decision-making process, the establishment of European Institutions, and a common monetary unit (with the Treaty of Maastricht in 1992) denote otherwise. However, it is neither a Federal Union, as most countries preserve their sovereignty, significant control over the national actions, set up individual priorities and strategies, even when interacting with Union members. The created conditions are not perfect. It is true that all the nations decide the general degree of integration. However, a larger number of members and the contradiction in their visions got harder to manage. It was evident during the United Kingdom leaving the EU after the Brexit sentiment grew stronger, propelled by the argument of the EU's regulative reach.

This factor alone creates dissonances and technical divergences between states. Adding the variation in economic performance, industrial specialization, existing infrastructure, and cultural factors only deepen the divide. Application of policy includes EU, national and regional levels, increasing the complexity for comparison and assessment. It is crucial to understand these principles before embarking on any EU policy, strategy and actions analysis.

At its core, the EU is still an Economic Union. The EU's four mobility pillars (free movement of goods, services, capital and persons) heavily hint in that direction. Therefore, as a Macro-regional, continental and global economy, it strives to maintain its competitive position worldwide. It is in tight economic rivalry with other macro-regional forces, such as the United States, Japan, Singapore and China (Lundvall and Borrás 2005; Trading Economics 2022). To do so, the Union understood that its competitive status depends on the potential to innovate and support innovations (European Commission 2006). Despite the aforementioned obstacles, the EU remains an important player in establishing policy and setting up strategic vectors for its members. It is also true in the context of the Innovation policy, which is developed to help the Union's countries grow their potential in a meaningful way and sustain a general vector for all the members.

The innovation policy in the EU has a long history that can be tracked from the member states' cooperation with OECD (Lundvall and Borrás 2005) and the beginning of the European Research and Innovation programme in 1984 (European Union 2019). With the Strategy of Lisbon, it became a critical issue for the EU's economy. The focus on innovation is rather high, as it was a priority for the EU development until 2020 (European Commission 2010). However, it was not included in the following strategy. The priorities for 2020–2024 were set on the green transition, digitalization, sustainable and democratic economy (European Union 2022b). Still, innovation plays the merging role between all the strategic visions and, most importantly, serves as the means to achieving the EU's agenda. Therefore, innovation can be considered a core concept for the EU's development, not only as an economic player but also as a social union and a political construct.

One of the leading principles in the Innovation policy in Europe was the Open Innovation Approach (European Parliament 2016). During the period of Europe 2020 strategy, the innovation field's latest policy area was the triple Openness approach (European Union 2019). This was a major commitment of the EU members to the idea of expanding the innovation potential and enriching it through Openness at internal and external levels (Bogers, Chesbrough, and Moedas 2018a), especially in contrast to previous policy focusing more on the internal market (see European Commission, 2006). The current revisions in 2022 (European Commission 2022f) follow most of the parameters set in the previous formulation (2014–2019). The so-called 3O's had a deep impact on the strategy of European innovation.

Since the EU strives to sustain its competitive potential and achieve sustainable development for its citizens through innovation (Skivko 2021), the policy should be well written and properly carried out. There is no denying that implementation is the key aspect of any strategy. However, policy evaluation plays a critical role in acknowledging results, understanding the strengths and weaknesses and setting up further platforms. This is why the mechanisms of policy assessment should be well tailored to the aims and adequately measure the results. A valid and reliable tool is imperative to the self-assessment and efficient policy implementation, ensuring that the goals were reached. The most known tool of Innovation

Assessment in the EU is the European Innovation Scoreboard and its addon, the European Regional Innovation Scoreboard (European Union 2022c). It captures the innovation potential and innovation-relevant parameters for the EU member state and subnational regions in the EU. Therefore, the Scoreboard collects data and highlights a unique score that indicates the innovation performance in the European framework.

In this context, the chapter aims to understand the connection between policy and its assessment. The chapter is not focused on commenting on the efficiency of the applied methods, collection of data and other technical aspects related to policymaking. The main goal is to understand whether the available means of comparing Innovation performance in the EU is adequate to measure the general implementation of the Union's Innovation Policy. It will consider the European Innovation Scoreboard (European Union 2022c) and the EU Policy on Research and Innovation (European Commission 2014). Although a particular example, it can illustrate how the EU institutions are promoting economic visionaries and coordinating their efforts. Thus, it is also an exercise in observing the threads between the EU's mechanism of selecting and retaining discourses (Makarovič, Šušteršič, and Rončević 2014; Jessop 2010; 2004).

The innovation policy overview

In the EU context, the formulation and assessment of policy are taken seriously, especially considering the availability of indicators for the evaluation and genuine transparency (Pandiloska Jurak 2021). The same approach was taken with the idea of Open Innovation, Research and Science. Firstly, the policy aimed to combat some of the most prominent outcomes of the economic crisis of 2008, such as the slow GDP growth, unemployment and decreasing competitive edge on global markets. Secondly, the approach was to re-evaluate the structure of EU policy to empower the actors on the "application" edge of innovation. By turning the EU policy to a bottom-to-top slope, the policy reconsiders the funding projects, application bureaucracy, and risk reduction for radical innovation. And thirdly, a big step of the policy was to promote innovation as a soft concept in the Policy Formulation. This is seen through the intent of addressing the decreasing interest of citizens in science and increasing international cooperation and research ethics on all levels (European Union 2019). The policy pillars follow a general line, accessible and attainable by the Union as a community and not diving into the particularities of national areas. Still, the policy targets national patterns, provides consultancy mechanisms, and infiltrates the idea of innovation in the European framework.

Many of these aspects are not unique to the referenced policy. The intent to improve economic conditions and gain a competitive edge are common in numerous strategies. A particular aspect of the policy is the answer to global phenomena and acknowledgement of the changes in the innovation paradigm.

Setting up the context

The strategy acknowledges the genuine Openness of innovation on the international level (Herstad et al. 2010). The process was described based on Chesbrough's idea of erosion of a firm's boundaries, caused by the (international) workforce mobility and availability of private Venture Capital (VC). These processes make it difficult for enterprises to control the flow of proprietary information, expertise and know-how (Chesbrough 2003). But further, the development of the research competencies of universities, coupled with improved global knowledge circulation and rising competitive pressure between companies, had similar effects on the motivation to "open" the innovation process (Chesbrough and Vanhaverbeke 2011). As such, the Open Innovation theory (OI) suggests a shift in the paradigm of innovation application. It opposes the Close Innovation Model, that is, in utilizing internally developed technology and commercializing results of its own, usually linear, development of technology (Chesbrough 2003). The OI, however, rejects the premise that own knowledge is superior to the pooled information available in the firm's network or environment (Chesbrough 2003; Chesbrough and Appleyard 2007; Enkel, Gassmann, and Chesbrough 2009). In other words, companies must acknowledge that not all "brilliant minds work for them" (Chesbrough and Crowther 2006). Therefore, to maximize the potential for added value, a company has to consider integrating internal and external knowledge into the innovation and organizational architecture. Such a scenario is especially useful for companies that lack the necessary resources to engage in close innovation through Research and Development (R&D) (Spender et al. 2017; van de Vrande et al. 2009).

According to the OI practice, three main activities are associated with an open innovation concept. It includes obtaining, integrating and commercializing knowledge (West and Bogers 2014). At each level, there are various aspects for the private agent. For example, the searching procedure is associated with breadth and depth of technology and knowledge seeking (Laursen and Salter 2006). The concepts are associated with the source (breadth) and degree of technological absorption through searching (depth). Additionally, a company has to consider the application of knowledge and how much of the external sources it introduces to change internal processes. Some authors recommend that endogenous knowledge represents 2/3rds of the information and technology involved in innovation (West and Bogers 2014). As such, it is clear that additionally to innovation capital, OI activates managerial, organizational, human, time and other resources. The competencies to implement OI practices and the necessary assets can make it an "expensive" and maybe risky activity for Small and Medium Enterprises (SMEs) (Dahlander and Gann 2010; Laursen and Salter 2006).

In the context of knowledge absorption, the necessary skills to utilize external technology require even more effort. All of these mobilize additional managerial and technical resources in the company (Bigliardi and Galati 2016; Chesbrough and Appleyard 2007; Enkel, Gassmann, and Chesbrough 2009). Internal and linear innovation (such as R&D) provides necessary skills for the company, understanding what to search for, and comprehension of the adoption process (Chesbrough and Crowther 2006; West and Bogers 2014). Consequently, companies with closed innovation experience have an easier time considering OI practices. It proves that closed and open innovation are compatible rather than mutually exclusive. A company has to consider both patterns to achieve an optimal condition for innovation (Laursen and Salter 2006).

Companies can also access the innovation done via public research or in joint co-creation with a public body (Besednjak Valič, Kolar, and Lamut 2021; West et al. 2014). This enriches the available pool of knowledge for companies, offers the possibility to learn new innovation skills, and calls for additional attention to Universities and Knowledge-Creation Institutions from the policy perspective (Bogers, Chesbrough, and Moedas 2018; H. Chesbrough and Vanhaverbeke 2011). The application of external knowledge in the business sphere and the collaboration of private and academic sectors create additional pressures on such public players. Therefore, the evolution of Higher Education Institutions (HEI) and the extension of their societal roles (Audretsch 2014) can be explained through the shift to an open innovation paradigm.

In a practical sense, these processes allow companies to benefit in three ways: utilize external information, commercialize internal sources, and do both – use external and commercialize internal knowledge (West and Bogers 2017). This creates the main dichotomy of the OI practice and namely identification of innovation direction (van de Vrande et al. 2009). Inbound and Outbound innovation is the terminology used to differentiate between the direction of knowledge flow and technological utilization. When the information comes from outside (penetrating) the firm, such practices are called Inbound OI (Dahlander and Gann 2010; Papa et al. 2021). This is OI's "classical" aspect, utilising the available external technology and knowledge to improve internal competencies. In knowledge literature, it is similar to adoption and technology diffusion, when the companies implement the innovation existing in the environment. The Outbound OI applies to the process of capitalizing on existing internal knowledge by making it available in the market. Therefore, it might be through licensing or commercialization of information (Chesbrough and Crowther 2006). An additional example can include externalizing the paths to market when a company uses an intermediary to reach its customers. The latter is not as common as Inbound OI but gains more and more attention, especially with the development of new business models. As the theory progressed, the idea of OI was enriched with new practices that include the Inbound and Outbound OI divided into pecuniary and non-pecuniary practices. Ergo, companies have a matrix of four categories to consider for their action. These include Revealing, Selling, Sourcing and Acquiring knowledge (Dahlander and Gann 2010). Depending on the position within the network, relationship status and interest in the innovation process, companies can utilize different strategies to benefit. Even revealing offers necessary possibilities for community development and securing necessary relationships, especially in the value chains (West and Bogers 2014).

Consequently, the implication of Intellectual Property (IP) becomes obvious. The theory acknowledges its importance as a typical example of outbound OI, linking it to licencing technology (Chesbrough and Crowther 2006; Enkel, Gassmann, and Chesbrough 2009). On the one hand, Openness happens with the erosion of boundaries of a company and its ability to have control over its intellectual assets (Chesbrough 2003). Therefore, IP stays in the way of applying outbound and non-pecuniary strategies for a communal development or regional innovation system (Dahlander and Gann 2010). On the other hand, the concept of OI is in the possibility of companies benefiting from their knowledge and commercializing it. Thus, IP has the potential to create additional and auxiliary paths to market and business models. For a group of actors, and a wider perspective on innovation (e.g., local, regional), IP utilization contributes to knowledge diffusion and creation and provokes new ideas (Papa et al. 2021).

However, even IPR is not protecting companies from the risks of the OI practices. Licencing, sharing and co-creating knowledge makes companies vulnerable to outside actors. The possibility of displaying important architectural knowledge and other technology to partners can lead to them utilizing these assets for their benefit first (Dahlander and Gann 2010; Enkel, Gassmann, and Chesbrough 2009). Moreover, the management of OI practices comes in parallel with the application of routine tasks. Their concomitant status represents a serious effort for SMEs, making them divide the limited pool of resources and time (Bigliardi and Galati 2016; Chesbrough and Appleyard 2007; Enkel, Gassmann, and Chesbrough 2009). It is especially complicated for them to manage the IP framework (van de Vrande et al. 2009). Therefore, the utilization of OI practices does not guarantee a big jump in the competitive and innovation race. The managerial and organizational resources necessary to implement OI are high and sometimes complex for SMEs, explaining the prevalence of closed innovation patterns (Bigliardi and Galati 2016).

These risks are not indicating that Openness is an undesirable strategy for private actors. OI benefits SMEs and allows them to compensate for the lacking resources for linear innovation (Spender et al. 2017; van de Vrande et al. 2009). Therefore, applying OI practices shall come with an understanding that it is not a "panacea" solution for the economic agents and their environment. Therefore, the decision-making and policy formulation have to consider the optimal solutions to guide networks to adequate innovation strategy. Herstad et al. (2010) underline the importance of using three types of tools to improve policy efficiency in a globally opening innovation. In their view, the policy-makers benefit from three main types of actions: a) That focus on the intramural R&D to increase the internal capacity for adoption; b) That focus on the creation of local links to promote knowledge circulation; and c) The ones that focus on the development of a balanced connection with local and foreign partners. These tools are to be considered contextually, accounting for the locational particularities. For example, supporting internal R&D must trigger the incentives to integrate external knowledge for indoor linear innovation. This points to the necessity of sustaining a balanced pool of information sources. The approach is supported by the perception of Laursen and Salter (2006), who argue that the relationship between open search and performance creates a concave curb, where insufficient and excessive reliance on OI harms the process.

Henry Chesbrough and Wim Vanhaverbeke (2011) also published a list of recommendations tailored for the EU in applying the Open Innovation Policy. Their approach consists of five main points – a) Enhancing education and human capital – including principles of research funding and promotion of mobility and exchange; b) Funding OI practice – by increasing private VC and promoting spin-offs to commercialize new technology; c) Considering the IP framework – by reducing costs, promoting the growth of intermediary partners to reach markets, and enhancing the diffusion of technology from HEI; d) Enhancing cooperation and competition – by shifting the innovation focus to help SMEs and not big companies, including through spin-offs from university research and bigger corporations, and promoting heterogeneous cooperation; e) Expand Open Government – as focusing on the transparency and accessibility of public data, reconsider the public procurement and support the investment of private capital in public technology development. Similar to the previous list, it includes aspects that are not directly related to the OI practices but target internal processes that can be transferred outside or integrated inside the firm or environmental conditions that trigger Openness. For example, investing and promoting human capital coincides with many aspects of creation, searching and integrating knowledge. Combined with expertise mobility, one of the factors causing the dissolution of the close model, it enhances the potential of companies to adopt and create new knowledge by combining internal and external know-how. Promoting collaboration and heterogenous linkages is a common factor in these views. Expanding the pool of information sources induces further erosion of firm boundaries and application of the OI model. Altogether, these are intended to strengthen almost all innovation practices, from R&D to entrepreneurship and to public-private co-creation. In this regard, OI highlights that all innovation processes are important, and Openness only indicates the possibility of using more alternatives. All mentioned encompasses the questions of social entrepreneurship (Kleindienst 2019) and gained skills (Ljubotina 2021).

Getting to know the 3O's strategy

Acknowledging the transformations in the innovation process, the European Policy adopted the vision of three-levelled Openness. The strategies in this approach are Open Innovation, Open Science and Openness to the World (European Union 2019). In a general sense, the pillars target the aspects tangential to the OI practices, being consistent with the policy recommendations listed in the previous sub-chapter. As such, Open Innovation policy actions consider the application of Smart Public Investment, which is to compensate for the risks of venture capital and private investments in innovation; Engaging in Heterogenous cooperation between businesses, users, researchers and citizens; and Optimization of Regulatory Environment, to guarantee efficient and science-based policy formulation, implement bottom-to-top development through programmes and reducing their bureaucracy. Its main approach is to stimulate social involvement in the innovation process, making it accountable for the current challenges. Open Science focuses on increasing accessibility to academic work such as publications (e.g., Journal Articles); promoting transparency and access to Public Data-Sources; and strengthening the ethics and practice of research through (heterogenous) collaboration and mobility. This approach ensures the diffusion of information from the public sector, strengthening collaborative research and infrastructure. Finally, the Open to The World focuses on extending the policy and engaging non-EU stakeholders. It targets international cooperation on emerging global issues, which justifies the metaphor of "science as foreign policy." Still, this pillar intends to propel cross-border research, share risks and promote joint interests. It mirrors previous recommendations for OI practices, operating on the premise of widening external sources of knowledge. Engaging non-EU countries in the research programmes and EU funds was a significant step in collaboration with EU neighbours.

The pillars are supported by additional actions and milestones (see Table 9). One of the main aspects of its implementation was the idea of focusing on social challenges and problems as the main focus of research and innovation activities. This fosters resources and soft skills to improve innovativeness and social conditions through them. This fosters resources and soft skills to improve innovativeness and social conditions through them. The approach was transposed to the 2020–2024 policy, where innovation is also the means to achieving the EU agenda (European Union 2022b). Such an approach has a practical side to these pillars. Other actions target research and policymaking conditions to appropriate the innovation practices. Horizon 2020 is one of the main tools identified by the policy in this regard. Some of the actions directly target the programme's application to enhance its outputs and accessibility. Others are set to optimize the existing regulatory framework to include and standardize European Members' actions.

The 3O's policy is indeed more focused on the Openness of certain innovation activities, especially over the EU borders, but in many factors is continuing its predecessor. For some time, and before the acceptance of the 2014–2019 strategy, the EU struggled to create enough business-targeted research, generate enough venture capital and support Intellectual Property creation compared to its global competitors, such as the United States or China (Chesbrough and Vanhaverbeke 2011; European Commission 2006). Therefore, the previous policy similarly focused on promoting the education system and boosting digitalization skills. The intent to strengthen the research and innovation potential through smart funding is pursued as well. The idea of optimizing, standardizing and reducing bureaucratization of EU policy at the level of member states is also present and targets mainly similar goals (European Commission 2006). The main difference was the focus on internal markets in 2007–2013 and the visible switch to enclosing non-EU skills and expertise for the policy of 2014–2020. Both focus on boosting cooperation between stakeholders but support different means. The 3O's policy tries to reproduce actions leading to erosion of the closed innovation system, while the strategy of 2006 is oriented toward the Cluster and Regional Innovation Systems approaches (Gangaliuc 2022). In a general sense, it continues the initiatives of previous policy. Nevertheless, it readdresses some aspects, such as heterogenous cooperation, and guides them into a new innovation paradigm.

The legacy of 3O's approach can be seen in the most recent innovation strategy of the EU (European Commission 2022f). Many of its actions continue or are tangential to the milestones set in 2014. It touches on the issue of improving private investment, taxation and venture capital environments. Both consider the importance of the funding Programmes for innovation development, especially in public procurement. Either understand the need to improve the infrastructure for research and knowledge diffusion, alongside the need to promote the interest in science and enhance soft innovations skills. The main difference in the policy action is the leaning of the new strategy on creating frameworks for radical novelty, deep-tech and the importance of diversity and equity in the innovation process. And to some degree, the approach comes back to promoting regional innovation systems and linking them within and outside the EU. It is not a negation of Openness, as it associates both approaches, emphasizing the importance of SMEs and open practices simultaneous with regional specialization. The plan of linking regional ecosystems only strengthens the idea that Openness had a big impact on the development of European innovation. The OI paradigm is clear in such regard, especially as the policy focuses on strengthening the co-creation and co-development of technology through collaboration between regions. Moreover, the 2022 policy builds upon the idea of integrating foreign experts into the EU pool of knowledge.

Many parameters can be seen in all three generations of policy. For example, the practice of optimization and reduction of bureaucratization of regulations is a common aspect of all these strategies. It is not to say that the policy formulation is redundant, but rather to acknowledge that the EU focuses on implementing state-of-the-art solutions and not letting development be stopped by outdated visions. Similarly, continuous checking and optimization of regulative frameworks are important given the status of the EU. As a unitary market, having an inimical national policy that is not accounted for a common standard can jeopardize Union's economic development. Additionally, it highlights the intent of the EU officers to build upon the work of the previous generation of strategies. The intent to keep good practices and only tailor them to modern needs is hardly a bad approach. Therefore, it activates the mechanism of selection and retention of visions on the Union's level (see Jessop 2004; 2010).

The innovation assessment tool

The European Innovation Scoreboard (EIS) is a comparative instrument developed for monitoring the Member States' innovation performance. It is augmented by the Regional European Innovation Scoreboard (REIS), which considers the 240 NUTS 2 regions of the Union (European Union 2022c). The concept was introduced After the Lisbon Strategy in 2000, where the innovation was acknowledged as the engine for the development of the EU economy (European Parliament 2000). The performance is measured as an underweight average of a series of indexes, reflected as the percentual equivalent for the performance of the EU. This is especially emphasized in the EIS' definition of four innovation groups: Innovation Leaders (more than 125 % of EU average), Strong Innovators (between 100 % and 125 % of EU performance), Moderate innovators (between 70 % and 100 %), and Emerging Innovators (less than 70 %) (European Commission 2021f; 2021b). The platform also considers a comparison against the benchmark of the innovation performance in 2014, allowing an analysis over time.

In 2001, the EIS published its first annual report on the innovation status quo. The measurement had 18 indicators focusing on human resources, development and diffusion of knowledge and the available funding. Therefore, it included parameters representing the (tertiary) educational background, public and private investment in R&D, development of IPR, venture capital, digital skills and the cooperation patterns of SMEs (European Commission 2001). Since then, the tool has been revisited several times. The backbone of the assessment is present, but it was enforced with additional indicators, and, in 2021, it counts 32 comparative points (European Commission 2021f; 2021e). As the webpage suggests, the changes are done with the intent to make the Scoreboard reflect the EU's political visions (European Union 2022c).

In the last decade, the Scoreboard underwent three changes – in 2014, 2017 and 2021 (represented in Table 8). These changes are significant compared to the initial set of indicators. Additional parameters quantify the direction of Eco-Innovations (the position [No.] 36–38), the progression of digitalization in the innovation (e.g., positions 8, 9, 17 and 18 added after 2017), and the soft skills and innovation efficiency measurements (e.g., counting expenses per employee [16], and job-to-job mobility [24]). These examples only reinforce the conclusion that the EU is interested in promoting adequate policy and offering the possibility to identify its efficiency. Consequently, it does lead to the retention of socio-political and cultural visions (see Makarovič, Šušteršič, and Rončević 2014; Pandiloska Jurak 2021; Jessop 2010; 2004) even in the assessment of innovation.

The Scoreboard is not without its limits. It operates on data available through Eurostat, and, thus, some national statistics are not synchronized with the tool (European Commission 2021f; Bielińska-Dusza and Hamerska 2021). It is even worse for the REIS, whereas many data are not collected for the regional level. Additionally, studies found that not all the indicators contribute to the overall index. According to Bielińska-Dusza and Hamerska (2021), five parameters show no correlation with the Summary Score. These include the SMEs performing internal innovations (position 21), Co-publications of public and private stakeholders (23), the number of Patent Applications (26), Private companies providing ICT training (17), and the per cent of Foreign Doctorate Students (7). Alongside these, there are objective questions of whether other indicators are relevant in the context of innovation, if the summary index is valid in assessing innovation[1], and others.

Author's representation based on the European Innovation Scoreboard Methodology (European Union 2014; 2017; European Commission 2021e; 2021f; 2021b). R= Removed. A= Absent.

In a practical sense, the EIS is a credible tool widely used for analytical and policy needs. The four categories of innovation countries/regions might not be perfect but are very well perceived and adequately reflect the established economic realities. It is to mention that the assessment of the innovation performance includes direct results and activities associated with the innovation process. Most of these parameters are included in the "IMPACT" section. Other segments are coping with environmental factors enabling innovation. It is especially true for the human skill and cooperation capital. Moreover, it also considers the linear and non-linear models of innovation, measured through "INVESTMENT" and "INNOVATION ACTIVITIES" modules.

Despite its criticism, the EIS achieves its main goal. As being focused on the Member States comparison (which also includes a few non-EU countries such as Bosnia and Herzegovina, Israel, Norway, Switzerland, Macedonia, Serbia, Turkey, Ukraine and its former member, the UK), it offers a good perspective on the case-to-case analysis and following the evolution of one country.

Comparing the 3O's strategy and the European Innovation Scoreboard

To examine the compatibility between the Innovation Strategy 2014–2019 and the EIS, the chapter considers the extended Policy Actions and Milestones (European Union 2019) and all the indicators present between 2014–2021

---

1 This is especially important given the unsettled dispute on the nature and process of innovation. Moreover, it raises the question if an average and summary value measures the Innovation Systems, as the Lisbon Strategy intended for it. Systemic particularities can create some relevant output without relying on all of the practices listed in the EIS. Thus, the innovative output will not be represented by the index in an adequate way.

Table 8: Innovation Scoreboard comparison

Type	No.	Measurement Framework	2021	2017	2014
FRAMEWORK CONDITIONS					
Human Resources	1	Doctorate graduates per 1,000 population aged 25–34	✓	✓	✓
	2	Percentage of population aged 25–34 having completed tertiary education (30–34 in 2014)	✓	✓	✓
	3	Lifelong learning, the share of the population aged 25–64 enrolled in education or training aimed at improving knowledge, skills and competences	✓	✓	A
	4	Percentage of youth aged 20–24 having attained at least upper secondary level education	R	R	✓
Attractive Research System	5	International scientific co-publications per million population	✓	✓	✓
	6	Scientific publications among the top-10 % most cited publications worldwide as percentage of total scientific publications of the country	✓	✓	✓
	7	Foreign doctorate students as percentage of all doctorate students (non-EU in 2014)	✓	✓	✓
Innovation-friendly environment/ Digitalization	8	Broadband penetration (Share of enterprises with a maximum contracted download speed of the fastest fixed internet connection of at least 100 Mb/s)	✓	✓	A
	9	Individuals who have above basic overall digital skills	✓	A	A
	10	Opportunity-driven entrepreneurship	R	✓	✓

(Continued)

Table 8: Continued

Type		No.	Measurement Framework	2021	2017	2014
INVESTMENTS						
Finance and support		11	R&D expenditure in the public sector as percentage of GDP	✓	✓	✓
		12	Venture capital expenditure as percentage of GDP	✓	✓	✓
		13	Direct government funding and government tax support for business R&D	✓	A	A
Firm investments		14	R&D expenditure in the business sector as percentage of GDP	✓	✓	✓
		15	Non-R&D innovation expenditures as percentage of total turnover	✓	✓	✓
		16	Innovation expenditures per person employed in innovation-active enterprises	✓	A	A
Use of ICT		17	Enterprises providing training to develop or upgrade ICT skills of their personnel	✓	✓	A
		18	Employed ICT specialists	✓	A	A
INNOVATION ACTIVITIES						
Innovators		19	SMEs introducing product innovations as percentage of SMEs (*Product or Process in 2014, 2017*)	✓	✓	✓
		20	SMEs introducing business process innovations as percentage of SMEs (*Marketing or Organizational in 2014, 2017*)	✓	✓	✓
		21	SMEs innovating in-house as % of SMEs	R		
Linkages		22	Innovative SMEs collaborating with others as percentage of SMEs	✓	✓	✓
		23	Public-private co-publications per million population	✓	✓	✓
		24	Job-to-job mobility of Human Resources in Science & Technology	✓	A	A
		25	Private co-funding of public R&D expenditures	R	✓	✓

Category	#	Indicator			
Intellectual Assets	26	PCT patent applications per billion GDP (in Purchasing Power standards)	✓	✓	✓
	27	Trademark applications per billion GDP (in Purchasing Power standards)	✓	✓	✓
	28	Individual design applications per billion GDP (in Purchasing Power standards)	✓	✓	✓
	29	PCT patent applications in societal challenges	R	R	✓
IMPACTS					
Employment Impacts	30	Employment in knowledge-intensive activities as percentage of total employment	✓	✓	✓
	31	Employment in innovative enterprises	✓	✓	
Sales Impact	32	Medium and high-tech product exports as percentage of total product exports	✓	✓	✓
	33	Knowledge-intensive services exports as percentage of total service exports	✓	✓	✓
	34	Sales of new-to-market and new-to-enterprise product innovations as percentage of total turnover	✓	✓	✓
	35	License and patent revenues from abroad as % of GDP	R	R	✓
Environmental sustainability	36	Resource productivity	✓	A	A
	37	Air emissions in fine particulates (PM2.5) in Industry	✓	A	A
	38	Development of environment-related technologies	✓	A	A

(enumerated based on Table 8). As the perspective of the EIS changes, it is important to consider that the tool was used to potentially target some of the policy aspects.

Even at first glance, it is clear that not all the practices can be represented from a statistical perspective. Many policy goals target the regulatory framework and the mechanism of policymaking. The overall status of such actions cannot be assessed via national or regional statistics targeting innovation performance. On the other hand, particular indicators can be affected if the policy is well implemented. Therefore, the comparison considers the importance of indirectly linking the indicators with policy actions and formulated goals to indicate the potential compatibility. In other cases, the comparative frame acknowledges that certain actions can target the Policy specifically (indicated as Policy Target). Some might have tangential relationship to national innovation performance (marked with Not Measured). The latter refers specifically to implementing the Horizon 2020 programme, such as to promote newcomers and gender equality among applicants. The comparative analysis is summarized in Table 9:

Table 9: The comparative table of 3O'S strategy and EIS

3O's Policy Actions	EIS Parameters (No. in Table 8)
Tackling Societal Challenges through Science:	
Targeting Social Challenges through R&I and H2020	29*; 36*, 37*, 38*
Interdisciplinary R&I through mission-driven research.	11, 23, 25, 29
Expand H2020 on exceptional projects that exceed budgetary constraints	[Policy Target]
Increase research funds	11, 13, 25
Improve Researcher's Skills through Mobility and Training (and links to the private sector)	1, 2, 3, 4, 5, 6, 9, 17, 18, 24
Strengthen research infrastructure (increase funding)	1*, 11
Connecting and Strengthening Institutions, especially in lagging areas	1*, 2*, 7, 11,
Funding breakthrough innovation:	
Creating Venture EU and European Innovation Council	10*, 12, 25, 34*
Extend the synergy with EU strategic investment and EU Regional Development Funds	[Policy Target]

Table 9: Continued

3O's Policy Actions	EIS Parameters (No. in Table 8)
Shifting resources to market-creating innovations through SMEs and entrepreneurship	10, 12, 19, 20, 21, 22*
Reforming funding schemes – simple and competitive approach	[Policy Target] 14*, 15*, 16*
A single rule for Tax incentives to promote Private R&I investment	13 (to monitor)
Democratizing research and innovation:	
Open Science Policy Platform and Open Science Monitor	8*, 23*
Open Access for EU-funded research, helping with the dissemination of knowledge	8*, 23*, 33*
Creating a digital infrastructure for Data baking	[Policy Target]
Promote High Standards for Research	2, 3, 5, 6, 7, 30*, 31*
Modernizing Copyright Regulation to allow the creation of disruptive digital knowledge	8*, 9*, 17*, 18, 28, 29*, 30, 33, 35
Involving citizens in science (particularly through H2020)	1, 2, 3, 4,
Making EU funding more Bottom-up	[Policy Target]
Promote Mission-Based R&I that benefits Citizen Participation in Science	3, 23, 28, 29
Increase Gender equality in science through H2020	[Not Measured]
Increase the percentage of newcomers in H2020	[Not Measured]
Improving Policymaking and Reducing Bureaucracy:	
Optimize and make Science-Based Policy Formulation Mechanisms	[Policy Target]
Reflect and promote Ethical Implications in Research	[Policy Target]
Launch H2020 Policy Support Facility	[Policy Target]
Making EU Regulation more innovation Friendly	Could affect: 12, 13, 14, 15, 16, 19, 20, 22, 25, 31, 34, 35
Incorporate the Innovation principle into EU policymaking	[Policy Target]
Launching the second eave of simplification of programmes and policy	[Policy Target]

(Continued)

Table 9: Continued

3O's Policy Actions	EIS Parameters (No. in Table 8)
Boosting international cooperation and science diplomacy:	
Improving the framework of cooperation between EU and non-EU countries	5, 6, 7
Strategic partnerships on global problems (food, climate change, etc.)	37, 38
Attracting exceptional non-EU researchers to the EU's pool of talents.	7
Use science as means to help and strengthen relationships with global partners.	5, 6, 7, 37*, 38*

Table Source: European Union 2019; *= indirect appropriation (e.g., the number of PhD students can be affected by the investment in research).

It is to acknowledge that some of these matches might be subjective, some missing or unclear. However, it is easy to observe that the policy and the assessment tool are going hand in hand in many aspects. Most of the principles are covered, at least indirectly. For example, the first row, on targeting social challenges through science, cannot be directly assessed. However, knowing that the EU has set its political goal to reduce pollution sets it as a social challenge and thus is measured through the ability of a country to develop and introduce eco-friendly technology (36, 37, 38). Similarly, patenting such solutions (29) will also represent an indicator of the policy action implementation. Therefore, the degree of fitness is not perfect concerning many actions, but it grants a genuine preview of the consistency and efficiency of EU policy implementation.

The indicators that were not evidently related to any policy action are the ones reflecting the IPR framework of Patent (26) and Trademark (27) applications and the parameter indicating the percentage of high-tech production exports (32). Nevertheless, these are very much in line with the 3O's and further the new 2022 policy goals. The difference is that some specific actions might target or preferentially consider some forms of IP (in this case copyrights) and not be as focused on patents and trademarks. Similarly, the perception of High-Tech exports resembles the intent of the policy to increase digital competencies. Moreover, it is in line with the new (2022) plan on enhancing deep-tech innovations and digitalization. The main difference is in the aspects of assessing exports, which are not directly treated by the policy and can only indicate another indirect match.

In general terms, the compatibility between Strategy and Assessment tools is not wondering. Not only because these are supposed to be in line with each other and EIS makes an effort to correspond, (European Union 2022c), but also because both are following the recommendations set by the literature. It is especially evident considering Chesbrough and Vanhaverbeke's (2011) points. The Policy and the EIS heavily emphasised the development and strengthening of Human Capital and Resources to secure necessary skills and engagement. In the case of 3O's policy, it is via the involvement of citizens in the innovation process and simultaneously boosting the capacity and quality of researchers. For the EIS, it is via capturing the number of educated, trained and skilled personnel that contributes to the innovation environment. Moreover, both focus attention on the funding streams, VC, research grants and other financial resources, which is the second recommendation. The Policy and EIS capture the IPR framework, making it secure to protect IP while simultaneously advantageous to use external knowledge. And finally, each of them considers cooperation patterns (less so competitive pressures) and the governmental competencies relevant to the innovation process.

Part II. Achieving the 2030 sustainability goals: Case studies

5. UN sustainable development goals 2030: Industrial Symbiosis within the European policy assessments

Sustainability is currently globally considered a backbone of political, economic and social strategies for carrying out any production activity, necessary to be able to face the harsh tests of global warming. The traditional economic systems, based on the utilization of natural resources, are the primary reason for environmental catastrophes, which grow even more severe every year. Spectacular technological and economic advancements seen in the "short century" are what have enabled people to live in better conditions, reduce global hunger, and ensure resources of wealth and care. We are faced with demographic growth and the population predictions are in expansion by 2050. With this, the consumption of natural resources is linearly expanding, which means that the linear economy reaches the highest limits. Besides, the growing industrialization has also led to amplified resource use and carbon dioxide emissions, which are largely responsible for the increase in GHG emissions. With the knowledge and technology in recants years, new perspectives have gradually opened up to transform the production paradigms. Systems of SD structures changed the processes, guaranteeing a significant reduction in costs of raw materials water and energy. Regardless, the EU is already active for many years in establishing favourable regulations, directives, policies and strategies for the transition of companies and industries into environmental efficiency. This plan of the European ecological transition is the EGD which was taken as a reference point for the new NGEU and therefore also for the NRRP. The EU has to face some more factors within the mentioned plan, such as a significant amount of resources must be given, and projects necessary to reactivate the economic framework and drive the growth of dejected areas must be initiated. Within the research, we briefly underline some *main concepts* in the sustainability of IE: CE and EIP with the emphasis on the IS development and its main policy implementations within the EU. The European policies attract increasing attention to the conceivable role, that IS could show in the changeover to industrial circularity and effectiveness, especially now within the implementation of EGD (Fric 2019; "A European Green Deal" 2022). After the Covid-19 recovery and the NRRP capability, the EU propose an exclusive chance to accelerate the IS growth. Despite all, it always stacks when we speak about money. MS of the EU should aim to make not only more adaptable funding structures but also political support, competent organs at all levels, and centralization of lawful and relief taxes to gain as much as possible from the IS approach (EU Cohesion Policy implementation in Slovenia 2020; European Commission 2022m).

Policies towards concept of the Industrial Symbiosis

Starting with the basic concepts; IE is a scientific discipline that studies the interrelationships between the companies – "the industrial metabolism" (Ayres 1989) of the IE and the environment in which the human system is expressed at a social, productive and cultural level. CE is defined (MacArthur 2013) as one of the leading establishments in the field of sustainability, according to which it is "a generic term to define an economy designed to be able to regenerate itself". In a circulating economy, the flows of materials are of two types: "the biological ones, capable of being reintegrated into the biosphere, and the technical ones, destined to be revalued without entering the biosphere" (MacArthur 2013; European Commission 2015c).

IS – the concept was first time used in 1947, defined by George Thomas Renner as "the set of exchanges of resources between two or more dissimilar industries" (Renner 1947, 167–189). Different authors define IS in varying ways, such as an approach to IE (Džajić Uršič 2020a); a synonym for IE (Phillips et al. 2006, 242–264); a subset of IE (Chertow and Lombardi 2005); an activity in IE (Rui and Heijungs 2010); an Eco-IS which represents local or regional CE and environmental approach (Chertow 2007; Howard-Grenville and Paquin 2008, 157–175; Gingrich 2012, 44–49; Hartard 2008). One of the levels of studying IE (Hartard 2008). Deutz (Deutz 2014, 3–13) sees IS as a stream of available resources (including water, energy, and materials), starting with firms that would have useless resources, and ending with actors that use these resources as new resources. Some are also attempting to be recognized as environmentally aware of their social environment (Costa and Ferrão 2010, 984–992; Costa, Massard, and Agarwal 2010, 815–822; Eilering and Vermeulen 2004, 245–270). When discussing the IS in literature, there are many times used synonym EIP or EIP network instead of IS, but there is a noticeable difference between terminology, still, because the measure and space of the aims, players involved, and practices are different (Winans, Kendall, and Deng 2017). The distance between industries, energy, and material flows between entities is the most critical factor because the initiatives from EIP include exchanges of water, energy, information, and or materials. We all are committed to using less energy and raw materials, and reducing waste, in order to build sustainable economic, ecological, and social relationships (Winans, Kendall, and Deng 2017). While IS network evolved with the same idea as EIP but covers a broader geographic area within a region, a province or a country. Regarding the organizational aspects, there are three main models for the development of an IS system (Džajić Uršič 2020a): IS districts, EIP, and ISNs. In the first two cases, there is greater stability of the symbiotic mechanisms, while in the third, the constraint of the relationships between the companies is lighter, and therefore the symbiotic relationships can change over time and space (European Commission 2015c). As said all that, IS can then be seen from two points of view, one from the IE and the second from the point of CE. Here is taken into account the CEs' point of view, where IS can be framed as a vital archetype of the business model based on the sharing of infrastructures and by-products to improve resource efficiency and create value from waste (Džajić Uršič 2020a; 2020b).

Policy development

The EU Circularity support the SD and can be considered the source of an present and future economy. Regarded the concept that Sum and Jessop develop in his book (Sum and Jessop 2013) in present case, all policy bullet points of EU Circularity are to be retained in a way to reinforce the selected discourses. Therefore, in compliance with the commitments taken in environments of cooperation and international confrontation, such as the UN and its institutions, the EU has proved to be an organization extremely sensitive to requests for environmental protection, developing large strategic plans aimed at initiating the ecological transition of the continent and financially supporting its implementation (Miotto 2021).

Since the 1980s, the EU has been concerned about ecology. At that time, the EU was the first political and economic organization to have extensive knowledge of environmental policy and was therefore seen as a benchmark within a global framework (Braun 2016). The Single European Act contains the first formal mention (1987) and is an unquestionably crucial text for European political cooperation since it formalizes and defines a beginning regulatory framework, to ensure the sensible use of natural resources while also protecting the environment and human health. Subsequently, the Maastricht Treaty (1993) makes the environment an official sector of EU policy and the Treaty of Amsterdam (1999) establishes the obligation to integrate environmental protection into all sectoral policies of the EU to promote SD. In 2009 the Treaty of Lisbon supposes that fighting climate change (European Commission 2021a) and pursuing SD in interactions with third parties, are particular goals of the Union. This gives the EU a new legal personality, enabling it to negotiate international agreements from that time (Kurrer 2021; Miotto 2021). Miotto (Miotto 2021) summarize the position of the EU, which has taken on the regulatory and policy level, as follows: "the EU policy on the environment is based on the principles of precaution, as stated Miotto (Miotto 2021), preventive action and correction at the source of data caused by pollution, as well as on the "contaminator pays" principle. The multiannual environmental action programs set the framework for future action in all areas of environmental policy (Miotto 2021). They are integrated into horizontal strategies and are taken into account in international negotiations on the environment topic (Kurrer 2021; Miotto 2021).

From this point of view, one can see how the European model has undoubtedly promoted ecological initiatives. After following the Lisbon Treaty, the EC outlined the essential strategies for EU MS regarding the issue of SD. EC set important objectives to be achieved in a period which, according to the propositions, ranges from a few years to a few decades, to transform the economic system in the direction of SD (Miotto 2021). Some of these strategies came out as follows by Eckert and Kovalevska (2021):

- 2010: "EUROPE 2020: a strategy for smart, sustainable and inclusive growth";
- 2011: the "EU biodiversity strategy up to 2020";
- 2015: the "The missing link – EU action plan for the CE";
- 2018: the "The EU's Plastics Strategy aiming to transform the way plastic products are designed, manufactured, used and recycled in the EU";
- 2019: the "Directive (EU) 2019/904" (Miotto 2021).

In the context of the CE, the EC has also paid particular attention to the issue of the bioeconomy, which, already examined within the program Europe 2020, is more explicitly stated in the plan established in the document "Innovation for sustainable growth: a bioeconomy for Europe" of action COM/2012/060 final (European Commission 2012a). The plan of this action focuses above all on the need for investments, in research and technological development activities and the sector to increase its economic weight. In 2018, this program was updated (European Commission 2018b). Observing the crucial role of the bioeconomy for SD, the EU launched in 2019 a series of 14 concrete initiatives concerning the EU priorities (European Commission 2018c). The EC suggests expanding the bioeconomy's footprint by spreading it locally, especially close to major cities to increase its environmental impacts. In light of this upgrade, "to be successful, the European bioeconomy must have sustainability and circularity at its centre (Miotto 2021). This will guide the renewal of our industries, the modernization of our primary production systems, the protection of the environment and the protection of biodiversity"(European Commission 2020d). Eckert et al. (Eckert and Kovalevska 2021) stated that already taken planning undoubtedly contributed significantly to the initial concrete measures taken toward the ecological transition, but the goals have only been partially met, and the economic structure has not undergone a fundamental change (Džajić Uršič 2020a). This is because of the global recession and the sovereign debt crisis, whose consequences have been made worse by austerity measures, especially in the uncompromising nations, and which have caused a significant slowdown in the economy and the investments that would have been required for a more profound SD.

Industrial Symbiosis as a tool in the middle

IS concept, as a resource efficiency model is now a part of the 17 SDGs issued and adopted by all UN MS in 2015 (European Commission 2015a). The mentioned SDGs are part of The Agenda 2030 for SDG adopted by Resolution 70/1-Transforming our World on 25th September 2015 (United Nations 2015). It provides a shared design for the sake of world peace and prosperity, approaches to the discrepancy, requires policies that enhance health and education, reduces inequality, promotes economic growth, fights climate change, and works to protect our oceans and forests, now and in the future. The 17 SDGs and 169 targets adopted by the Agenda 2030, which are an urgent call to action for all nations – developed and in development – in a global partnership, are at the centre of it. After adopting the SDGs, The Agenda 2030 started to have a decisive role in structuring targets and convergences among EU policies.

The Paris Agreement and the framework of the SDGs served as the foundation for the EGD, which was announced publicly by the EC on 1st December 2019 (European Commission 2015d).

EGD established the areas where the goals of achieving climate neutrality by 2050 should be attained. The EGD established the foundation for activities to be taken by national governments and carried out by businesses, individuals, and organizations, taking into account the difficulties and targets for emissions reductions and carbon neutrality in light of two significant milestones: Agendas 2030 and 2050 (Koundouri, Devves, and Plataniotis 2021; European Commission 2022b).

They establish six priorities for the years 2019–2024, among them two, in particular, are considered pillars for the future of the EU: the implementation of an EGD and the digital transformation of the economy.

The EC, therefore, promotes a double transition, digital and ecological to modernize the economy of the EU. Thanks to greater competitiveness, and free growth from the constraints of fossil fuels. The Agenda 2030 and associated SDG are therefore functional to the implementation of the EGD. It turns obligations from EC into a great opportunity, to make the European economy and society global leaders in ecological production and the well-being of citizens (European Commission 2022b).

After the EC published the EGD document (European Commission 2019a) it stated that EGD is: "the initial roadmap of the policies and the main measures necessary to achieve the EGD" and "a new growth strategy aimed at transforming the EU into a just and prosperous society, with a modern, resource-efficient and competitive economy that in 2050 will not generate net emissions of GHG and in which economic growth will be dissociated from the use of resources" (European Commission 2019a). The EGD is based on four pillars of diplomacy: *trade, bilateral financial agreements, multilateralism through the UN, and domestic implementation of its »Fit-for 55 climate package«* – an EU ambition, committing to cutting emissions by at least 55 % by 2030 (European Commission 2019a).

In March 2020 (European Commission 2020c), the EC announces the "new industrial strategy for Europe" with which the EC intends to propose a new direction for European industry that is fully in line with the EGD's requirements. The strategy targets industrial ecosystems and their value chains directly, emphasizing a competitive and non-protectionist system while also being mindful of global challenges and their potential to cause economic distortions. Security in terms of the availability and accessibility of clean energy and raw materials, as well as industrial innovation, whose development will be hastened thanks to resources made available through public-private partnerships, are the main goals for European business. However, the Covid-19 pandemic starts to spread quickly throughout EU MS and the rest of the world in the same month, having a severe effect on society and the economy owing to deaths and lockdowns. This results in a temporary slowdown of the EGD's implementation timeline, however as will be later described, the EC has a path to recovery – NextGenerationEU (NGEU) (Miotto 2021).

Relating to the UN SDG 2030, IS is more close to the Goal12 (responsible production and consumption) which finally indicates the achievement of Goal 9 (industry, innovation and infrastructure) and Goal 13 (climate action). At the same time as offering the essential economic growth to achieve Goal 8 (decent work and economic growth) and Goal 11 (sustainable cities and communities). The inevitable consideration that IS phenomena (Džajić Uršič 2020a) is a very complex approach with this wave effect, makes it very important in the achievement of all 17 Goals, and it could be merged and applied in all industry sectors including social organizations.

Within the IS, the EGD sets up the agenda to make like a normal business attitude, where the initiatives (local and regional) are on ongoing action and aim to attract small and medium enterprises with the contribution to forward moving local and regional development and attractiveness. And here is the duty of the European policy to integrate IS in constant reviews of regulations, that cover the whole value chain. Nevertheless, IS has established successful closing the resources loops and moved waste up the value chain, so secondary raw materials and by-products are becoming a feasible substitute for the use of primary raw materials within this approach (Sommer 2020). A wide range of Regulations and Directives acknowledge the importance of IS itself, while some crucial strategies as the Resource Efficient Europe Flagship Initiative under the Europe 2020 Strategy, the CE Action Plan, EU Waste Framework Directive, … Some of these strategies aim at delivering policy's transformation of the production systems, business models, technology, funding, abilities, and civilian behaviour (Sommer 2020).

EU policies have well-defined guidelines, on how will be the best way to engage in practices, and contribute to climate neutrality in a way of waste prevention and reutilisation. On the other side, the consideration of companies and stakeholders are more focused on processes as recycling and waste treatments. Still, the effective IS development, placement of (green) technologies, innovation, incorporated industrial strategy and strong governance agenda strengthened the whole CE system. Challenges such as finances, the creation of marketplaces, low-carbon energy, and non-energy sources for climate neutrality should be at reasonable prices. On a global scale, IS has been applied with recognised environmental, economic, and social benefits. For example, »the highest number of IS initiatives in Asia can be found in China and Japan, mainly because of national policies on carbon dioxide emission reduction and national encouragement of CE practices« (CircLean 2022). Since the 1970s, IS has been active in North America, remarkably in the pharmacological area. Brazil, Algeria, Australia, and Morocco are countries, where the cases of growing IS applications have been registered (CircLean 2022). Despite not having (yet) a directly dedicated action plan on IS, the EU actions consider the interlinkages between *value chains, employment, innovation and eco-innovation* within IS. As similar, the EU policy includes aspects that moreover laterally or directly support IS within pollution and waste, resource effectiveness, material security aiming at reducing foreign dependence on certain raw appurtenances, as well as including new areas of climate and environmental issues (e.g., climate adaptation and mitigation), green employment and invention, and eco-innovation (CircLean 2022).

Besides the growing number of policy examples that are supplementary to national, regional, and local IS in the EU, there is a pioneer case: the Kalundborg (Denmark), which is considered one of the earliest and most famous examples of IS in the world. It began in 1961 in town Kalundborg in Denmark, as a water management project (Fric 2019; Ehrenfeld and Gertler 1997). Kalundborg is a small harbour town on the northwest coast of the largest Danish island of Sjælland in Denmark. IS case Kalundborg has been subject to extensive scientific research by scholars of industrial ecology and organizational management (Džajić Uršič 2020a; Fric 2019). It has, however, long been a unique phenomenon and various attempts to copy it have failed. Here the Nordic countries have this division on IS strategic policies very well divided (Finland – SITRA National Roadmap for CE in Finland and West coast of Sweden – Sotenäs Industrial Symbiosis Network). The support from national and regional levels in Finland, Sweden, Denmark, and Norway has played a big role in linking cross-border collaborations, getting together research institutes, small and medium enterprises and industry clusters, which contribute to the development and implementation of the EU long-term grand strategies policies: sociological, policy, and regional considerations of The Agenda 2030 and IS policies within EU (Sommer 2020). Despite Kalundborg is worth mentioning the "National Industrial Symbiosis Programme" (NISP), which can be regarded as the first systematic blueprint approach toward the widespread implementation of IS (Bruck 2016). It has already been exported to various countries worldwide . NISP has risen to become the benchmark in the creation of IS networks, as much, as countries like France and Finland have already begun to adopt the concept by launching they're national IS programs (CircLean 2022).

The EU sustainable recovery towards Industrial Symbiosis concept

The EC has been monitoring IS in Europe, reflecting a range of segments, such as the economic profitability of reducing cost by processing waste, new sales produced, destruction and waste management, reduction of landfill resources and consequences for green (GROW.DDG1.C.4 2016; Baas 2011; European Parliament and European Council 2015). Eco-innovative models are stimulated to identify economic and social profitability (Joyce and Paquin 2016), customer behaviour and the products' environmental consequences (Daddi, Nucci, and Iraldo 2017). Also, other key elements of the IS have to be considered the environmental, such as impacts of products, the legal aspect of the collaboration, the role of public and government institutions (Costa and Ferrão 2010) and specific features of sustainability (Chun and Lee 2017).

Considering EU policies is inevitable to mention tools, that represent concrete policy measures used to implement policy objectives and targets in strategies. These are regulation (laws, rules and directives that are obligatory and where disobedience often will be sanctioned), economic and market instruments (incentives, where public authorities dampen or encourage certain economies by creating e.g., taxes or e.g., subsidies), relation and capacity building instruments (soft policies, voluntary and non-forced) (Kettunen et al. 2018; Bemelmans-Videc, Rist, and Vedung 2017).

The EU aims to be climate neutral by 2050, with an economy with Zero net GHG emissions in the EU. This target is related to an objective of the EGD and in connection with the EU's duty to a global climate action, which is the heart of the Paris Agreement (European Commission 2015d). As in Table 10, we can list just some of the important policy milestones for the development and implementation of the SD in the EU.

Table 10: Roadmap of EU policy documents

Release Date	Key Document
04/02/2010	EU Council on energy, Presidency conclusions
26/05/2010 -	Communication "Analysis of options to move beyond 20 % GHG emission reductions and assessing the risk of carbon leakage"
17/11/2010	Communication "Energy infrastructure priorities for 2020 and beyond – A blueprint for an integrated European energy network"
08/03/2011	Roadmap 2050 presentation in some Member States
08/03/2011	Citizen's summary: EU plan – low-carbon economy by 2050
08/03/2011	Climate change: Questions and Answers on a Roadmap for moving to a low carbon economy in 2050
08/03/2011	Climate change: Commission sets out Roadmap for building a competitive low-carbon Europe by 2050
08/03/2011	Energy Efficiency Plan 2011

(Continued)

Table 10: Continued

Release Date	Key Document
08/03/2011 – SEC (2011) 287 – SEC (2011) 288 – SEC (2011) 289	A Roadmap for moving to a competitive low carbon economy in 2050: – Evaluation of the online stakeholder consultation – Impact Assessment – Summary of the Impact Assessment
04/2012	Behavioural Climate Change Mitigation Options and Their Appropriate Inclusion in Quantitative Longer Term Policy Scenarios: – Main Report; – Transport Domain Report; – Housing Domain Report; – Food Domain Report; – Technical Report on the appropriate inclusion of results of the analysis in model-based quantitative scenarios
12/12/2015	The Paris Agreement is the first-ever universal, legally binding global climate change agreement, adopted at the Paris climate conference (COP21)
2018 – Vision for a long-term EU strategy for reducing GHG emissions	
28/11/2018	A Clean Planet for all – A European strategic long-term vision for a prosperous, modern, competitive and climate neutral economy
28/11/2018	In-depth analysis accompanying the Communication
28/11/2018	Press release: Commission calls for a climate-neutral Europe by 2050
28/11/2018	EU Visions: – Factsheet: Long-term strategy for GHG emissions reduction – Factsheet: Economic transition – Factsheet: Industrial transition – Factsheet: Societal transition
28/11/2018	– EU initiatives: – Putting the Financial Sector at the Service of the Climate – EU External Investment Plan – Opportunities for Africa and the EU Neighbourhood region – Urban Investment Support for Cities – Clean Energy for Islands Initiatives – Structural Support Action for Coal and Carbon Intensive Regions

Table 10: Continued

Release Date	Key Document
	– European Youth for Climate Action – Smart Finance for Smart Buildings Investment Facility – EU Rulebook for Investment in Energy Performance of Public Buildings – Investing in Clean Industrial Technologies – Clean, Connected and Competitive Mobility
28/11/2018	Supplementary information: data of the graphs presented in the in-depth analysis
11/2018 – 20/01/2019 – 20/03/2019 – 02/03/2020	Background report: Industrial Innovation: Pathways to deep decarbonisation of Industry – Part 1: Technology Analysis – Part 2: Scenario analysis and pathways to deep decarbonisation – Part 3: Policy Implications
/	Study: Review of technology assumptions for decarbonisation scenarios
17/07 – 09/10/2018	The public consultation
28/11/2018	In-depth analysis accompanying the Communication
03/2019	– Katowice climate package – The European Parliament endorsed the net-zero GHG emissions objective in its resolution on climate change
11/2019	European Political Strategy Centre study: "10 Trends reshaping Climate and Energy"
12/2019	The EU Council endorsed the objective of making the EU climate-neutral by 2050, in line with the Paris Agreement.
11/12/2019	A clear and complete repository of the thematic areas that are shaping the EGD (in a nutshell)
	Key documents from the Paris Agreement
06/03/2020	Long-term low GHG emission development strategy of the EU and its Member States
14/01/ 2020	Resolution on the EGD and Just Transition Mechanism
04/02/2020	– The EU submitted its long-term strategy to the UN Framework Convention on Climate Change (UNFCCC); – Proposal for a European climate law to ensure a climate neutral European Union by 2050; – Public consultation (open until 17 June 2020) on the European Climate Pact bringing together regions, local communities, civil society, businesses and schools

(Continued)

Table 10: Continued

Release Date	Key Document
04/03/2020	The first European Climate Law to enshrine the 2050 climate-neutrality target into law
10/03/2020	Adoption of the European Industrial Strategy, a plan for a future-ready economy
11/03/2020	Proposal of a new CE Action Plan focusing on sustainable resource use
20/05/2020	– Presentation of the EU Biodiversity Strategy for 2030 to protect the fragile natural resources on our planet – Presentation of the 'Farm to fork strategy' to make food systems more sustainable
08/07/2020 17/09/2020 14/10/2020 19/10/2020 10/12/2020 18/01/2021 24/02/2021 25/03/2021 12/05/2021 17/05/2021	– Adoption of the EU strategies for energy system integration and hydrogen to pave the way towards a fully decarbonised, more efficient and interconnected energy sector – Presentation of the 2030 Climate Target Plan – Renovation wave, Methane Strategy, Chemicals strategy for sustainability – European Climate Pact – European Battery Alliance – New European Bauhaus – New EU strategy on adaptation to climate change – Organic Action Plan – Zero pollution Action Plan – Sustainable blue economy
14/07/2021	Delivering the EGD
18/05/2022	REPowerEU plan: affordable, secure and sustainable energy for Europe

(Source: European Commission 2022a; Joyce and Paquin 2016)

EU existing sustainable indicators

Despite this and various authors' indexing, there is no singular indicator that can be used to measure IS or its growth, but a brunch of indicators and tools to monitor the transition to circularity. The EC uses a series of indicators at various stages for supporting policy-making, to facilitate monitoring results of the sustainability efforts and estimation including problem acknowledgement, policy formulation, decision making and monitoring realization as a mechanism of a vision selection (Sum and Jessop 2013). During the policy-making process, some of these indicators are newly developed and some existing indicators are just updated, depending on the supply of expressive information on social, environmental and economic questions (Adelle and Pallemaerts 2009; Yilmaz, Yontem, and Alkaya 2016).

The Directive (EU) 2018/2001 (European Parliament 2018) has established a series of indicators to monitor the transition to circularity and IS:

1. EU self-sufficiency for raw materials (%)
2. Green Public Procurement
3. Waste Generation
   – Municipal waste GDP
   – Generation of waste, excluding primary mineral waste, per unit of GDP;
   – Generation of waste excluding mineral waste for the consumption of household material (%)
4. Food waste (million tons)
5. Overall recycling rates:
   – Municipal waste recycling rate (%);
   – Recycling rate excluding major mineral waste (%)
6. Recycling rate for specific waste streams:
   – Overall packaging (%)
   – Plastic packaging (%)
   – Wood packaging (%) Electronic waste (%)
   – Organic waste (%)
   – Construction and demolition waste (%)
7. Contribution of recycled materials to the demand for raw materials
   – End-of-life recycling input rates (%)
   – Utilization rate of circular material (%)
8. Trade in recyclable raw materials:
   – Imports from non-EU countries (tons)
   – Exports to non-EU countries (tons)
   – Intra-EU trade (tonnes)
9. Private investment, jobs and gross value added (European Commission 2018d):
   – Gross investments in tangible goods (% of GDP)
   – Persons employed (% of total employment)
   – Value added at factor cost (% of GDP)
10. Number of patents related to recycling and secondary raw materials (European Parliament 2018).

Despite indicators, various tools for measuring sustainability (environmental, economic, social) have been developed to support the sustainability objectives and environmental assessments for example Life Cycle Cost, Life Cycle Assessment, the ecological footprint, the environmental sustainability indexes, the measurement of net savings, material input per unit service, environmental risk assessment, material flow accounting, cumulative energy requirement analysis, input-output analysis, total cost accounting, Cost-benefit analysis,.. (Hák, Moldan, and Dahl 2012; Ness et al. 2007; Singh et al. 2007; Herva et al. 2011; Roca and Searcy 2012).

EU funding systems towards sustainable developments

The EC supports public funding systems in multitudinous areas, such as Directorate for Industrial Technologies, recently renamed Substance which is simultaneously funding about 350 systems in the EU (European Commission 2020b). To look productively at these unknown funding challenges, it's essential to ensure a harmonious and coordinated frame of the funding openings in EU, public and local positions, to attract private investment and to use taxation policy to support the perpetuation of low emigration results. Different EU funding programmes and instruments, including Horizon Europe, the Innovation Fund, the Connecting Europe Facility, and InvestEU should optimise their solidarity and complementarities. In June 2019, under the EC's Action Plan on Financing Sustainable Growth (European Commission 2018a) the technical expert group suggested a set of cost-effective actions, prepared in seven crucial sectors that can principally pay attention to climate change improvement. Nevertheless, this is the first step toward beginning an EU-wide taxonomy for environmentally sustainable conditioning to potentiate green investments (González-Val and Pueyo 2019). The action guide fiscal bodies, to measure the functioning of their investment and portfolios, to eventually justify green investments and GHG emissions. With the relinquishment of the EGD, the EU has put forward a clear roadmap with the ambition to come the world's first climate-neutral mainland by 2050. The most ambitious financed programme by now in the EU was the actual research and innovation framework programme (2021–2027) launched by Horizon Europe 2019 (European Commission 2016).

Subsequently, within the recovery plan of EGD, the EC in May 2020 propose NGEU, which is described by the same as "a temporary recovery tool of 750 billion EUR, that will allow the EC to obtain funds on the capital market, support mechanisms and financial resources for eco-innovation" from 2021–2027 (European Commission 2022c).

The NGEU was approved in July 2020 by the EC, following extensive negotiations. According to the EC, "this instrument will assist in repairing the immediate economic and social harm caused by the coronavirus pandemic, to develop a greener, more technologically advanced, robust, and more resilient post-Covid-19 Europe, adapted to present and future problems." The "device for recovery and resilience," a common fund with 723,8 billion EUR in it, of which 390 billion are grants to all EU MS, is the foundation of the NGEU (Staff and Eddington 2020). These funds are expected to be vital for the support of the EU's sustainable and resilient recovery, for creating jobs and renovating harms, that were caused by the pandemic Covid-19, while supporting the EU's green and digital priorities.

Some other investments are relevant by now, such as (1) ReactEU initiative, financed with 50,6 billion EU to be disbursed in the period 2021–2022, through which it will be possible to expand the measures against the crisis and further programs. One of them is InvestEU, dedicated to attracting private investments; (2) the EU long-term budget for the period 2021–2027, agreed by EU leaders also, is equal to 1074.3 billion EUR. It supports investments in the ecological and digital transition. All sum amounts from 2018, constitute a total of 1824,3 billion EUR, which, updated to current prices, rises to a package of 2018 billion EUR to be allocated within seven years to repair the damage caused by the pandemic and to make the European economy digital and sustainable (Directorate-General for Budget (European Commission 2021). Within the NGEU, the EU MS have to achieve four principles for SD: Green transition, Digital transition and productivity, Equity and Macroeconomic stability within the established budget and enhancing investment and the quality of public finances (Miotto 2021).

This year on 18th May, the EC published a REPowerEU plan on how the EU can eliminate its dependence on Russian fossil fuels, respond to rising energy prices in Europe and to replenish gas stocks for next winter. The EC quotes that delivering REPowerEU objectives demands an additional investment of 210 billion EUR from 2022–2027 (European Commission 2022g). The EC President Ursula von der Leyen said (European Commission 2022p): "We must become independent from Russian oil, coal and gas. We simply cannot rely on a supplier who explicitly threatens us. We need to act now to mitigate the impact of rising energy prices, diversify our gas supply for next winter and accelerate the clean energy transition. The quicker we switch to renewables and hydrogen, combined with more energy efficiency, the quicker we will be truly independent and master our energy system. I will be discussing the EC's ideas with European leaders at Versailles later this week, and then working to swiftly implement them with my team" (Borcharhardt and Christopher 2022).

6. Investing in the European Union economy – a focus on recovery policies for Romania

In a framework of almost of 20 years, the world has faced two major crises that affected the economic development of different countries, including the ones from the European Union. The first crisis, relates to the economic crisis from 2008. The second, the more recent, started in 2020 and related to the Covid-19 health crisis (Brada, Gajewski, and Kutan 2021). The economic crisis created problems in different sectors, though the effects were different due to the differences in national economies (Brada, Gajewski, and Kutan 2021). At the same time, Covid-19 health crisis, did not only affected world economies through Covid-19 infections and deaths, but also through the policy measures and announcements that the authorities made during this period. Last, but not least, the war between Russian Federation and Ukraine, is on the verge of starting a food crisis, Ukraine being in the top 5 countries of wheat exporters and energy crisis.

Crises from previous years that have occurred in Europe (as Brexit, nationalist movements, the refugee movements and especially the Covid-19 pandemic and the re-bordering measures) have reiterated the importance of the nation states in the border governance (Opiłowska 2021, 2). The previous mentioned crises, as the author states, can challenge the idea of a borderless Europe, thus making deterritorialization vulnerable to the challenges that appear. Nation states are having a forefront role in keeping the security. Thus, when there is a crisis, the nation state has the mechanisms in order to protect its interests, thus highlighting the fact that the practices of cross-border multi-level governance are considered and even more highlighting the fact that the state is a sole actor (Opiłowska 2021, 2).

According to the author (Guasti 2020, 48), during the Covid-19 Pandemic, democracies face bigger challenge from technocracy, plebiscitarianism and populism. Before Covid, technocracy could narrow the political competition and even more it can weaken the democratic accountability. For example, in technocracy, scholars point that most of the decisions are beyond the control of people. Populism, on the other hand even if weaknesses democratic process as technocracy does, the actions are different. Thus, populism can facilitate centralization (where there is a link between the populist leader and the people, rather than rule of the people) while transforming the political opposition into the enemy of the people, reduces the diversity of the public forum and weakens checks and balances. Lastly, the author (Guasti 2020, 48) mentions plebescitarianism, where it restrains the deliberative and participative elements of democracy and as a result undermines the division power. In this moment, the society transforms into passive viewers and the nobody can check how the leader rules.

Even more, the Covid pandemic, put more pressure on democracy, while it was facing problems in several European countries. As a result, the three aspects mentioned earlier, can negatively contribute to this process. On one hand, technocracy during the Covid time can strengthen the role of virologists and epidemiologists and to certain extent it can undermine accountability. On the other hand, in populism, different political actors can use the pandemic as an excuse to strengthen the exclusionary rhetoric and weaken institutional safeguards. Lastly, in plebiscitarianism, there is the risk of wakening the roles of the parliament, opposition and civil society (Guasti 2020, 48).

Thus, as a result, it can be stated it can be stated that the Covid pandemic does not only represent a threat for the public health sector, but to democracy. There is a possibility that the state of emergency to be used to expand the executive power and enable temporary curbs on civil liberties with the argument of helping the public health sector. Nevertheless, as the author points (Guasti 2020, 57) there are preconditions for democracy to remain untouched. Firstly, it is important for the press to critically assess the information that is gets from the government. Secondly, the judicial system must ensure that all measure and restrictions remain in the constitutional framework. Thirdly, it is highlighted the role of the opposition, which must be effective in monitoring the government. Lastly, the civil society must defend democratic principles.

As a result of the crises that are happening not only on the European continent, the European Union, has come-up with a recovery plan (European Commission 2021d) which aims to address the consequences of the pandemic and help to improve and transform European Union national economies, but also to tackle the aspect of democratic decay.

Overall, the presence of competing strategies is a normal process in a democratic society. Thus, it is important to look at these strategies not only through the lenses of simple strategies, but rather understand them as part of a larger framework that can explain the prevalence of certain strategies over the over. In order to have this understanding, we can look at the Cultural Political Economy theory, which integrates four important mechanisms of analysis. As Jessop and Oosterlynck (Jessop and Oosterlynck 2008) point-out, competing discourses on sub/supranational or macro levels, pass through: variation, selection, and retention and reinforcement. Each of them, representing an important step in policy formulation and implementation.

Relying on publicly available document and data, the aim of this chapter is to address the Recovery Plan for Romania, in order to see the key actions that

Romania will have to implement, in order to reduce the effect of current crises on the European continent.

The socio-economic development in the European Union

The socio-economic development is an aspect that most of the countries provide support. As This is a result of the transformation of modern economies to global ones (Akimova et al. 2020). Even more, it is linked to the need to ensure sustainable development of the territories. When it comes to the European Union and the planification of the territories' socio-economic development, according to the authors in the literature there are several indicators that that to be considered:

- employment of population
- economically active population
- average life expectancy of the population
- indicator of agricultural labour
- the number of enterprises actively engaged in activities.

Thus, as the authors consider, all regional development programs must have the EU's principals as:

- to ensure territorial integrity, which must be more balanced socio-economic development of the regions, because of the need to increase their competitiveness;
- to provide the improvement of the rural-urban relationship, thus it will contribute to the development of regions;
- to modernize the connections between cities and villages;
- to ensure that information and knowledge is available;
- contribute to the preservation of the environment by reducing the negative impact on it;
- the protection of natural resources and natural values must be strengthened;
- cultural heritage must be increased, because it contributes to the development of the territories
- a rational use of energy resources (Akimova et al. 2020, 569).

Regional Cohesion Policy

Through the Cohesion policy, the European Union has one of its objectives, the reduction of the social and economic differences in the Union. Additionally, this policy comes as a help to the policies that are already on the national levels. Thus, this policy allows regional policies not to act in terms of disintegration (because of free movement and differences in a large competitive environment), because of its integration(Gavril and Nae 2019, 288). Even more, as the authors, the Cohesion policy aims to address poorer regions by offering them the necessary tools to improve their productivity growth and potential growth, thus contributing to redressing the existing regional disparities. In other words, the aim is to increase the demand for goods and services. This can be achieved through investment and at the same time reduce catching-up by investing in human capital and infrastructure.

As the authors point (Akimova et al. 2020, 570) the strategy of the European Union is to pursue regional cohesion, thus contributing to the harmonization of the European Union region development. More detailed approach is laid down in the Strategy "Europe 2020", which has the aim to focus on several important actions:

- the promotion of regional growth. The aim is to increase the regional competitiveness, especially focusing on those that are less developed
- the promotion of inclusive growth. It can be achieved not only through the employment increasement, but also through the improvement of quality of life and well-being of the population focusing on environment, namely by its protection and quality upgrading (Akimova et al. 2020).

When it comes to countries with transition economy, e.g. Poland and Romania, according to the of the analysis of socio-economic development features of rural territories in European Union Member States, such countries implement various measures to improve socio-economic development of rural areas. Meanwhile, other countries that are considered to have transition economies, according to the authors, should consider Poland's and Romania's good practice and focus more on rural areas (Akimova et al. 2020, 573). Poland and Romania are regarded as countries that have intensified their activities toward strengthening the rural areas, though the implementation of different mechanisms in order to improve the socio-economic development in the above-mentioned area.

Romania

For Romania to increase integration through achieving economic competitiveness and sustainable development, it must increase its absorption capacity of structural funds. Thus, these funds will help in the creation of jobs, improve the environmental conditions, sustainable economic growth, thus contributing to increasing the living standard of the population (Gavril and Nae 2019).

As the authors stress, Romania has the need in focusing on areas as rural development, agriculture, education, infrastructure and health. Considering that these areas are important, because of the issues that Romania is encountering, the Cohesion policy can be a regarded as an opportunity to contribute to the economic development and the reduction of inequalities and regional differences (Gavril and Nae 2019, 288).

When Romania became a EU member state, along its status of a EU country, it inherited the possibility to shape the EU regional policy according to its interests. Nevertheless, at the same time, this possibility was burdened by its poor development of the administrative-institutional capacity, thus influencing the absorption capacity. As the authors point (Gavril and Nae 2019, 293), one of the characteristics that the absorption community funds require, is the combination of several administrative and legal framework aspects as: good inter-ministerial and inter-institutional coordination and effective management, coherent legislative framework, efficient administrative structure. Even more, the stakeholders have to follow several phases: programming, implementation, monitoring and evaluation. Thus, as a result of having weaknesses in administrative capacity, limited budget available for co-financing or lack of strategic milestones, resulted in uncertainty, especially among local authorities, related to the absorption capacity. Nevertheless, for Romania, the cohesion funds focused on competitiveness, technical assistance, regional development, agriculture and fishery, cooperation administrative capacity human capital and infrastructure (Gavril and Nae 2019, 294–295).

Recovery plan

The Covid-19 pandemic affected all member states of the European Union, but also all countries around the world (Mihailovici 2020). As the author points, at the same time all these countries have been affected differently their economies and social sphere. As a result, it can create an increase in differences of the Member States' economies or even the segmentation of the single market, because of the asymmetric capacity to absorb the pandemic consequences. Thus, the European Commission stressed the importance of a coordinated response at the European level (Mihailovici 2020, 15).

As a result of the consultations between the President of the European Council and European Commission and the member states, it was proposed a new Multiannual Financial Framework till 2027. This framework includes an instrument called – Next Generation EU (NGEU), consisting of 750 billion euros and has the aim to finance the European recovery over time short and medium time framework. Romania seeks to finance the national short-term recovery plan and long-term plan, though the process will be difficult. These difficulties are caused by the already existing budget deficits or pro-cyclical fiscal policy in times of strong economic growth. Nevertheless, one of the main challenges for Romania is the sustainable recovery of the economy (Mihailovici 2020, 15).

As the authors mention, the novelty of the newly created NGEU instrument relies on its financing, transfer mechanism, reimbursement source, duration, implementation, design and governance, rather than in the amount of money allocated (Mihailovici 2020, 19).

This new mechanism has the aim to guarantee the sustainable economic recovery. It will be done through the following objectives:

- convergence, through sustainable recovery;
- resilience, by improving economic and social structures;
- transformation, by the green and digital transition.

Thus, as the author mentions (Mihailovici 2020, 22–23), these objectives cover the following areas:

- renewable energies and clean hydrogen-based solutions;
- clean transport, (iii) food sustainability in a smart circular economy;
- infrastructure and digital skills;
- investment in future resilience crises;
- social protection;
- employment;
- education;
- research, innovation;
- health;
- areas related to the business environment, including public administration and the financial sector.
- sector.

Nevertheless, it is important to mention that as the author highlights (Mihailovici 2020, 30), as in case of prior of the pandemic, but also during the new scheme, these funds will be conditioned by a macroeconomic policy control mechanism. More specifically, Member States will submit to the European Commission the national recovery plan. This plan, as the authors point, must comprise a number of reforms and investments, which should follow the priorities set by the European Semester. At the same time, this plan must contain measure that will strengthen the growth potential, job creation and economic and social resilience in the specific country. Even more, a particular focus should be on digital transition and dual green. In the moment the plan is submitted to the European Commission, the EC will make the payment according the fulfilment of the milestones and relevant targets.

Recovery plan in action

In 2021 the Recovery plan for Romania was adopted. This plan (European Commission 2021c) sets a number of actions that the Romanian government has agreed to implement by the end of the programme. Thus, it comprises of both reforms and investment in the key component areas, which both the European Commission and the Romanian government, have agreed upon:

- Water Management
- Forests and Biodiversity Protection
- Waste Management
- Sustainable Transport
- Renovation Wave
- Energy
- Digital Transformation
- Tax and Pensions Reforms
- Business Support, Research, Development and Innovation
- Local Fund
- Tourism and Culture
- Healthcare
- Social Reforms
- Good Governance
- Education.

It has to be noted that the implementation of the reforms and investments in these areas that the Romanian Government has pinpointed, is expected till 2027. Nevertheless, it is important to mention that in order to have a smooth implementation of the reforms and investments, each of this component has a set of indicators, milestones and indicative timeline for completion.

According to the European Commission's Summary of the assessment of the Romanian recovery and resilience plan (European Commission 2021g), the plan provided by the Romanian Government consisted in:

- 171 measures: 64 reforms and 107 investments divided into 15 components
- 507 Number of milestones and targets
- Climate target: 41 %
- Digital target: 20.5 %

According to the European Commission (2021c, 1), the proposed plan has the potential to enhance the socio-economic and institutional resilience and to increase potential growth. Even more, it can achieve recovery, which is the main target of the new programme. As a result, this plan is composed of six main pillars, which define and reinforce the reforms and investments to the areas, where the EU considers them as being primordial.

Namely, one of the pillars, results in focusing on the green transition. The emphasis is on the energy and climate measures, namely reforming the decarbonisation of road transport and phasing-out of coal. The unlocking of the renewable's deployment will be achieved through the reforms and investments. Even more, as the Commission points, these will decarbonise the energy sector. Additionally, there will be the need to consider the energy efficiency of both private and public buildings, deployment of electric charging infrastructures, digitalisation of road and rail transport climate change adaptation and circular economy. The concentration on these aspects, will contribute in achieving the green transition in all sectors of the economy.

Another important pillar that the Commission highlighted (2021c, 1) is the digital transition and has as aim to focus on the digitalisation of the public administration (including health, justice, environment, employment and social protection) and businesses, as well as connectivity, cybersecurity and digital skills.

Foster smart, sustainable and inclusive growth is also on the list of the pillars. Within the plan the are mentioned several measures that have the aim to realize the goal. Accordingly, among the measure the Romanian Government pointed that within the Recovery Plan, with the help of investments and creation of a National Development Bank, it will focus on:

- support private investments, including for small and medium-sized enterprises (SMEs);
- increase the capacity of the country to attract investments and create new businesses and jobs;
- reinforce fiscal sustainability through important reforms of the tax administration, tax framework, fiscal management and the pension system.

On other hand, by focusing on the structural measures on market and important reforms and investments targeting both urban and rural development, it will contribute to strengthen social and territorial cohesion. It expected that this mechanism will reduce territorial disparities at regional, intra-regional and intra-county level.

Lastly, it is aimed with the help of the reforms and investments to strengthen the resilience and digitalization of the health system. Even more, next generations are also at forefront. For this goal, the emphasis will be on the education system whereas there is the need to address aspects as quality, equity and infrastructure. Even more, in the moment in urban and rural areas the school and university infrastructure will be upgraded, the focus should shift also toward reducing the drop-out rate. Thus, it can be achieved through digitalisation of education and a system of grants.

Business support, research, development and innovation

As mentioned earlier the Recovery Plan tackles several key pillars that each of the European Union country focuses. Same aspect is valid for Romania. One of the kye component is Business Support, Research, Development and Innovation (European Commission 2021a, 287). The agreed component of the Recovery Plan includes a number of investments and reforms, which have the aim to strengthen the business milieu, research, development and innovation sector. In other words, it is expected to that this component will support firstly small and medium enterprises (though big businesses are also important) and organisations that are involved in research, development and innovation:

- Reform 1. Legislative transparency, de-bureaucratisation and procedural simplification for business
- Reform 2. Streamline governance of research, development and innovation
- Reform 3. Reform of research career
- Reform 4. Enhanced cooperation between business and research
- Reform 5. Support to integrate the research, development and innovation organisations in Romania in the European Research Area
- Investment 1. Digital platforms on legislative transparency, de-bureaucratisation and procedural simplification for business.
- Investment 2. –Financial instruments for the private sector
- Investment 3. Private sector aid schemes
- Investment 4. Cross-border and multi-country projects —Low Power Processors and Semiconductor Chips
- Investment 5. Establishment and operationalisation of Centres of Competence
- Investment 6. Development of Horizon Europe mentoring programmes
- Investment 7. Strengthening excellence and supporting Romania's participation in partnerships and missions in Horizon Europe

- Investment 8. Development of a programme to attract highly specialised human resources from abroad in research, development and innovation activities
- Investment 9. Support for the holders of certificates of excellence received in the Marie Sklodowska Curie Individual Fellowship Award
- Investment 10. Establishment and financial support of a national network of eight regional career guidance centres as part of the European Research Area Talent Platform.

The Recovery Plan points that these reforms focus on changes in the regulatory framework. The new regulatory framework will have the aim to simplify the legislation and to reduce the administrative burden for firms. Even more, the focus is on tackle the fragmentation and effectiveness of research and to improve the cooperation with the private sector or even to address the unclear governance (European Commission 2021a, 287).

Additionally, the changes are intended to create a digital platform, which has the aim to offer better public services for the business environment. For example, companies will have access to finances through financial instruments and grants. Even more, additional investments will support the research competence centres and research projects lead by internationally reputed researchers.

Lastly, this Plan is continuing the reforms and investments, which were conveyed for Romania in 2019 and 2021. Namely, it continues the reformation of the decision-making process (the country-specific recommendation related to the improvement the quality and predictability) and long-term projects in order to improve the competitiveness of the economy. At fore front is the integration of the local providers into EU strategic value chains and supporting research and development activities (European Commission 2021a, 287).

Innovation – a bridging point for Romania's Recovery Plan

It is important to point that the announced Recovery Plan is very ambiguous and has important aspects that could improve Romania's economic development. Thus, the European Commission highlights that it is important to prioritize, stabilize and increase the investments in the public and private investment in research, development and innovation and in physical and digital infrastructure (European Commission 2020e). These actions, are aimed to reduce the regional differences and to improve productivity and long-term growth. The Commission highlights that Romania is facing the risk for its competitiveness from two factors. The first one, the non-cost factors as the economy's low innovative capacity and poor institutional and poor quality of the infrastructure. These aspects hinder the possibility to compete internationally.

It is important to understand that the knowledge-based economy is dependent on research and innovation performance. These two indicators in case of Romania are weak, thus create obstacles for the process knowledge-based economy transition. Even more, as the reports point, Romania spend the least on research and development in the EU, which directly contributes to the level of science and diffusion of technology between the firms. Lastly, the Commission points that the support of innovative firms and R&D investment and quality, are at low levels, thus remain important challenges.

In the Innovation Union Scoreboard countries are dispersed on four levels of innovation development:

- emerging innovators;
- moderate innovators;
- strong innovators;
- innovation leaders.

A number of indicators are considered, when the innovation score is being composed. Thus, it is important to consider the complexity of the concept.

In 2020, according to the European Innovation Scoreboard (2020) Romania was catalogued as an emerging innovation. In comparison to previous years, Romania faced a decline in their level of innovation. For example, there was a decline until 2014, it was stable 2016 and with a slight increase during the 2017 – 2019 years (compared to the EU average). As the report, pinpoints, the strongest aspect of innovation is related to innovation-friendly environment and sales impacts. If we consider the EU average performance, then only high-tech product exports and broadband penetration can be highlighted. On the opposite pole, the weakest indicators are the human resources, innovators and form investments. Four indicators, which are the lowest, including the rest of the countries are: SMEs innovating in-house, Lifelong learning, SMEs with product or process innovations and SMEs with marketing or organizational innovations.

For 2021, the performance remained relative the same to the EU average. Nevertheless, the strengths and weaknesses noticed some changes in the indicators (European Innovation Scoreboard 2021). For example, as the strongest points for Romania relate to Sales impacts, Digitalisation and Environmental sustainability. Additionally, the top-medium Broadband penetration, Venture capital expenditures and Medium and high-tech goods exports. As the report pin-points also the fact that after 2020, there is an increase in Broadband penetration, Innovative SMEs collaborating with others, Most-cited publications,

Foreign doctorate students and International scientific co-publications. Lastly, it is important to mention that Romania shows a below average score on Climate change related indicators and above share of Non-innovators without disposition to innovate.

Innovation and Recovery Plan

As pointed, it is interesting to see where does Innovation comes at forefront in this particular component. Thus, the reference to innovation is present in three reform and in three investment proposals:

- Reforms – Streamline governance of research, development and innovation; Enhanced cooperation between business and research; Support to integrate the research, development and innovation organisations in Romania in the European Research Area
- Investments – Private sector aid schemes; Establishment and operationalisation of Centres of Competence; Development of a programme to attract highly specialised human resources from abroad in research, development and innovation activities.

Streamline governance of research, development and innovation

The main aim is to clarify and streamline the governance of the research, development and innovation system in Romania. The streamline governance of research, development and innovation will be achieved through the operationalization of the Policy Support Facility Reform Unit within the Ministry of Research and Innovation and Digitalisation. This Ministry will translate recommendations into reforms. Thus, these reforms will tackle national research, development and innovation ecosystem (European Commission 2021a, 293–294).

This reform is planned to take place till 2026 and will encompass the involvement of various stakeholders, where at stake is the reshape of the architecture and functions of the research, development and innovation system in Romania, but also to enhance the quality of investments. It is considered that it will create a permanent system where research, development and innovation policy across ministries and agencies is well designed and implemented. Additionally, it is expected that this reform to be sustainable even after the RRF timeline. Lastly, it is expected to have a special body with the aim to ensure the coordination between the ministries and in addition with private sector organisations coordination (European Commission 2021a, 293–294).

Enhanced cooperation between business and research

Another reform expected to be implemented is the need of enhancing cooperation between business and research. As a result, the aim is to create a favourable environment for both public and private investments through the cooperation of industry and research, development and innovation public research organisations.

It is planned to focus on contracting, financing, monitoring and evaluation of research projects with the help of simplifying and digitalising the legal framework. Another important aspect is the international evaluation before the approval by the Public Contracting Authority and ensuring open access to deliverables during the lifespan of the project (European Commission 2021a, 294). Namely, those deliverables that will be considered not sensitive and of great significance, will be made available to the scientific community and general public. Even more, it is expected to have a centralised electronic point of contact and create necessary conditions for stable and predictable sources of funding for research at the local and national level. Lastly, the Ministry of Research, Innovation and Digitalisation will cooperate with other decision-makers (e.g. Ministry of Education and its subordinated agencies, Ministry of Finance and Ministry of Economy) and improve the legal framework. Even more, the recommendations of the 2021–2022 Horizon Europe Policy Support Facility will be considered in the implementation of the above-mentioned actions.

Support to integrate the research, development and innovation organisations in Romania in the European Research Area

This specific reform focuses on the consolidation and increasement of public research, development and innovation organisations in Romanian, but also to integrate them into the European Research Area. Thus, the aim is to change the legal framework in such manner that it would encourage, facilitate and regulate the integration and merger of research institutions. Even more, the legal framework must set a periodic external evaluation of the performance of all research, development and innovation organisations in Romania. Even more, the aim is to have an impact on the social and economic levels. Nonetheless, the new legal framework must consider the recommendations of the 2021–2022 Horizon Europe Policy Support Facility. The amended legal framework will optimise the research work, by identifying potential mergers between research institutes. Even more, through a mechanism of periodic evaluation, research institutions will have access and non-financial support (European Commission 2021a, 294–295).

Private sector aid schemes

As in case of reforms, it is expected for innovation to be improved also though a number of investments. For example, there is expected to have an aid scheme for the digitalisation of SMEs. In other words, small and medium enterprises with the help of digitalisation will increase the competitiveness, contributing to innovation and new working patters. Nevertheless, the created environment will pressure SMEs to adapt to new digital realities, which is a key challenge for them. As the Plan points, the component's sub-investment offers two instruments to realise the above mentioned:

- a grant scheme to support entrepreneurs in development of advanced digital technologies (such as artificial intelligence, data and cloud computing, blockchain, high performance computing and quantum, internet of things, cybersecurity)
- a grant scheme of up to EUR 100 000 per enterprise to support SMEs adopting digital technologies (such as purchases of ICT hardware, development and/or adaptation of software applications/licences, including Robotic Process Automation software automation solutions, acquisition of blockchain technologies, procurement of artificial intelligence systems, machine learning, augmented reality, virtual reality, purchase of a presentation website, purchase of cloud and internet of things services, training of staff using IT equipment, advice/analysis to identify technical solutions that SMEs need).

A total of 500 millions of Euros are expected to be invested in this scheme (European Commission 2021a, 291–292). The leading position in the implementation of the reform, is offered to the Ministry of Investments and European Projects. Thus, the Ministry will elaborate a set of guidelines for projects. Additionally, the projects' monitoring will be delegated to an administrator with the obligation to monitor and report the progress of the project implementation. Nevertheless, the Ministry will supervise and ensure the managements and interfere in case there will be the need.

Establishment and operationalisation of Centres of Competence

The fragmentation of research, development and innovation organizations by supporting the implementation of Horizon Europe missions at national level are at forefront for this investment scheme. As a result, it is expected the creation of five "Centres of Competence". These Centres will focus on research activities that are in accordance with the Romanian and European strategic research priorities. It is expected to enhance the cooperation between academia-business collaboration in different primordial research fields. The collaboration will be achieved through the establishment of consortia off public and private research institutes and small and medium enterprises, with the aim to implement the Strategic Research and Innovation agenda. The joint projects will address the needs of local communities, thus contributing to the improvement the lives of citizens. Additionally, this creates a good opportunity to disseminate the results, upgrade the equipment and infrastructure (European Commission 2021a, 295–296).

Development of a programme to attract highly specialised human resources from abroad in research, development and innovation activities

Lastly, the development of a programme to attract highly specialised human resources from abroad in research, development and innovation activities will have the aim to increase the research capacity of the research development and innovation organisation. Thus, in other words, there will be granted 100 research projects by international researchers. The selection will be made based on an established criterion. These researchers must have research activity outside Romania in the previous three years. Additionally, they will be affiliated to host research institutions in Romania, thus through the attraction of funding, coordination project grant and funds, they will contribute to increase the research capacity of the host organisation (European Commission 2021a, 297).

7. Open innovation towards EU's Green Deal circular economy goals: Can the Covid-19 epidemic be an opportunity to accelerate the achievement of goals?

In 1972, it became obvious that European Union (EU) was already progressing economically but was still in need of a community environment policy so the European Council in Paris affirmed that such policy is required alongside an actionable program (Kurrer 2021). Since then, the Member States have embraced and implemented various environmental laws and regulations, resulting in the most extensive compendium of standards in modern times (Fric 2019). 40 years later and the environmental acquis of the EU consists of more than a thousand different directives and regulations. In this chapter we will mention *Directives* and *Regulations* and it is therefore practical that we clarify both types of legislative acts in the EU before continuing. According to the European Commission (2019a), Directive is a form of law specific for the EU and designed to impose obligations on Member States, however granting them the flexibility to consider their own legal and administrative traditions. Thus, each Member State can decide on their own how to align the Directive with the national legal and administrative system (European Commission 2019a). Although they are binding, some requirements in Directives may be modified according to Member State's environmental and economic conditions (European Commission 2019b). Regulations, on the other hand, do not allow Member States any flexibility and modification in their application as they are directly binding and supersede any conflicting national legislation when regulative provisions are not implemented through national law, even if the Regulation does not differ from the law itself (European Commission 2019b). Regulations are not implemented during legislative approximation phase but become directly binding only when Member States accede to them (European Commission 2019a). The core mission of the European environment policy is to caution, prevent and rectify negative environmental impact at the source and to ensure that polluters pay for their own negative impact – the 'polluter pays' principle (Kurrer 2021). According to the author, the multiannual environmental action program represents the framework for future actions in all areas of environmental policy as they are being implemented in horizontal strategies and considered in international environmental negotiations. After the release of the European Green Deal policy by the European Commission, environment policy has become the main driver of economic growth in the EU.

Over the past decades, European Commission's 306 policies and initiatives have brought about a high level of environmental protection in the EU by imposing EU legislation on international markets and requiring market players so keep up with its changes (European Commission 2019b).

Green transformation and EU environment policies will be effectively executed in the future with the help of green investment and mobilization of resources from Member States' budgets and the private sector. It is especially reassuring news that EU plans to allocate 30 percent of its 2021–2027 budget and 37 percent of Next Generation EU funding to climate action (Tagliapietra and Veugelers 2020). Circular economy is another such precondition for successful execution of EU environment policies, which at its highest conceptual level represents how the EU plans to deal with growing economies, limited resource consumption and environmental capacity (Ellen MacArthur Foundation 2019). The Circular Economy Action Plan, published in 2019 by the European Commission, lists activities that lead to lower carbon emissions, resource efficiency and competitive economies while at the same time ensure jobs, economic growth and investments. Although circular economy has become a global buzzword and is no longer only a trend but represents a modern way of living, the EU and other countries still have a long path ahead before plans turn into actions and its competitive advantage is fully evident in the economy (European Commission 2019c). The most obvious positive aspects of circular economy include providing new business opportunities and business models and developing new markets, not only within the EU but internationally. Much work remains to be done for the application of the updated waste legislation and on expansion of markets for secondary raw materials. On the other hand, certain actions enabling transition from linear to circular economy have already been put into motion on EU level but its execution will need to be accelerated for its effects to become visible (European Commission 2019c). Before that, however, it will undoubtedly also be necessary to carry out a critical-evolutionary analysis, as one of the concepts of cultural-political economy (Sum and Jessop 2013), to have a clear idea of the extent to which the measures introduced have been realized. Circular economy has proven to be very important for knowledge and technology transfer and especially for innovation, therefore its rapid implementation is vital. We also describe its impact in this chapter where we present one of the main paradigms named "*Open Innovation*" 2.0 (Fric 2022; Besednjak Valič 2022).

To return to normal after the Covid-19 epidemic, European Commission has envisaged certain scenarios with defined actions and guidelines for the continuation of activities for transition from linear to circular economy. In April 2022, five scenarios were published in a study titled *'After the new normal: scenarios for Europe in the post Covid-19'*. The study provides an overview of potential changes of the EU and its R&I policy resulting from the Covid-19 epidemic (European Commission 2022a).

While the momentum for action in circular economy transition at the EU level is intense and continues despite the Covid-19 epidemic, there are nevertheless several gaps. Therefore, the chapter presents the timeline overview of the ambitious legislative and legal framework for circular economy and open innovation – open innovation as one of the actions for shaping Europe's digital future, and circular economy as one of the actions for a cleaner and more competitive Europe.

We use the concept of Ellen MacArthur Foundation which describes circular economy process as a response to the pressures of a growing economy, consumption of limited resources and overall capacity of the environment (Ellen MacArthur Foundation 2020). In the second part, we focus on the crucial indicators, budget support, mechanisms and funding, comparing the status before and during Covid-19 epidemic, and, finally, try to answer the question: *Can Covid-19 epidemic serve as an opportunity to accelerate the achievement of goals?*

The timeline of circular economy legislation and actions: From the beginning to nowadays

Ellen MacArthur Foundation (2020) notes the concept of circularity has deep historical and philosophical origins. The idea of feedback, of cycles in real-world systems is ancient and has echoes in various schools of philosophy. It enjoyed a revival in industrialized countries after WW2 when the advent of computer-based studies of non-linear systems unambiguously revealed our world's complex, interrelated, and unpredictable nature. While the concept of a circular economy cannot be traced back to one date or author but rather to different schools of thought (Wautelet 2020), legislation in the field of circular economy at EU level officially started in 2015. A chronological overview of the key milestones which are crucial in the context of the chapter is given below (European Commission 2022a):

– December 2015: *First Circular Economy Action Plan* adopted by the European Commission.
– November 2016: Adoption of the Eco-design *Working Plan 2016–2019*.
– January 2018: *Circular Economy Package* adopted by the European Commission.

- July 2018: The revised legislative framework on waste enters into force.
- March 2019: Final *Circular Economy Package* adopted by the European Commission.
- June 2019: Revised fertilizer regulation enters into force.
- July 2019: Directive on single-use plastics enters into force.
- October 2019: Adoption of 10 Eco-design implementing regulations.
- December 2019: European Commission adopts the *European Green Deal*.
- March 2020: European Commission adopts *A New Circular Economy Action Plan*.

Even if the last milestone coincides with the start of the Covid-19 epidemic and then to nowadays, we do not see the new milestones as in the chronology before; this does not mean activities in this area are not being carried out. They are taking place in the domain of *A New Circular Economy Action Plan* for a cleaner and more competitive Europe. Therefore, we further focus on the last milestone, new circular economy action plan from March 2020, which is particularly crucial for this chapter, especially as it is one of the building blocks of the European Green Deal.

As emphasized by the European Commission (European Commission 2022d), *A New Circular Economy Action Plan* is one of the crucial building blocks of the *European Green Deal*, Europe's new agenda for sustainable growth. EU's transition from linear to circular economy will reduce pressure on natural resources and will create sustainable growth and jobs. It is also a prerequisite to achieving the EU's 2050 climate neutrality target and halting biodiversity loss. *A New Circular Economy Action Plan* announces initiatives along the entire life cycle of products. It targets how products are designed, promotes circular economy processes, encourages sustainable consumption and aims to ensure that waste is prevented and the resources used are kept in EU economy for as long as possible (European Commission 2022d).

European Commission (2022b) explicitly emphasizes that transition from linear to circular economy is the most important engagement of all target groups – industry, policy-makers, businesses (especially SMEs), HEIs, and NGOs as stakeholders in the civil society. The mentioned approach of a *New Circular Economy Action Plan* is going to provide stakeholders with a systemized framework to foster partnerships across different sectors (Džajić Uršič 2020a; Džajić Uršič 2020b). Finally, the transition from linear to circular economy also requires active engagement of citizens in changing consumption patterns.

To ensure that the period during Covid-19 epidemic (except for activities, such as events) did not have an impact on the stalling of activities in the domain of *A New Circular Economy Action Plan*, we describe below the activities performed from the emergence of Covid-19 epidemic to nowadays (European Commission 2022d):

- December 2020: European Commission adopts a proposal for a new regulation on sustainable batteries.
- February 2021: Global Alliance on Circular Economy and Resource Efficiency launched.
- October 2021: European Commission adopts a proposal to update rules on persistent organic pollutants in waste.
- November 2021: European Commission adopts a proposal for new rules on waste shipments.
- March 2022: European Commission adopts a package of measures proposed in the circular economy action plan.
- April 2022: European Commission adopts proposals for revised EU measures to address pollution from large industrial installations.

Furthermore, the European Parliament in February 2021 adopted a resolution on the new circular economy action plan demanding additional measures to achieve a carbon-neutral, environmentally sustainable, toxic-free and fully circular economy by 2050, including tighter recycling rules and binding targets for materials, use and consumption by 2030 (EU Monitor 2022).

In addition, the European Commission in March 2022 proposed a package of legislative measures under the European Green Deal, which were previously announced in the Circular Economy Action Plan. The aim of the legislative package was to make almost all physical goods on the EU market more sustainable and thus more environmentally friendly, circular and energy efficient throughout their entire life cycle, from the design phase to daily use, reuse, and end-of-life (EY Global 2022).

In this domain, the European Commission proposes four crucial initiatives (EY Global 2022):

- The Eco-design Regulation for Sustainable Product;
- A working plan for eco-design and energy labelling for 2022–2024 period;
- Amendments to the Consumer Rights Directive;
- Unfair Commercial Practices Directive.

Together, these proposals aim to make sustainable products the norm – more energy efficient, greener and more circular overall. With the proposal for a Regulation on Eco-design the European Commission would replace the Eco-design Directive to broaden the current range of non-energy related products and to extend the scope of compliance requirements. The aim is to achieve more circularity by making products more durable, reliable, reusable, upgradeable, repairable, easier to maintain, refurbish and recycle, and more energy efficient (EY Global 2022). The circular economy is, therefore, a paradigm shift based on the reduction, reuse, recovery and recycling of materials and energy, replacing the linear concept of end-of-life. The circular economy goes far beyond waste, waste management, and recycling are, above all, a catalyst for competitiveness and innovation (BIN@PORTO 2018). In the context of this chapter, it is innovation that we see as the driver for implementation of circular economy and so we focus on it below.

Enforcement of transition from linear to circular economy is crucial cooperation in the field of knowledge and technology transfer and a lot of innovation – especially innovation – in practice and in the domain of this chapter where we present one of the crucial paradigms – 'Open Innovation' 2.0 (Fric 2022). Mentioned is also noted by Jesus and Jugend in their research. The main findings are (Jesus and Jugend 2021):

- Utilization of open innovation within the circular economy is still a recent phenomenon, one which emphasizes the collaboration between stakeholders and the co-creation approach.
- Collaboration of stakeholders can be applied to align the objectives of interested parties in a joint effort to resolve the environmental problems of the three levels of circular economy.
- An action-creation approach can be adopted as a strategy to encourage the participation of consumers in the development of environmentally sustainable products which may favor the transition to the circular economy.

In this chapter is 'Open Innovation 2.0' (OI2) understood as a new paradigm based on a *'Quadruple Helix Model'* where government, industry, public research organizations and civil stakeholders work together to co-create the future and drive structural changes far beyond the scope of what any one organization or person could do alone (Fric 2022). OI2 is a positive innovation approach that helps solve critical European challenges by embracing change and not resisting it, financially supported predominantly by Europe 2020 flagship initiative (Fric 2022).

The timeline of open innovation legislation and actions: From the beginning to nowadays

Chesbrough (2006) and EURIS (2012) notes 'Open Innovation' as a new paradigm which assumes organizations can and should use external ideas as well as internal ideas and internal and external paths to market as the organizations look to advance their technology (Chesbrough 2006; EURIS 2012).

While 'Open Innovation' is a model based on the premise that organizations can benefit from free bi-directional flow of ideas and innovations from both within and outside the organization, it is also much more than an open version of open innovation (Morikawa 2016). OI2 is a new paradigm based on principles of integrated collaboration, co-created shared value, cultivated innovation ecosystems, unleashed exponential technologies and extraordinarily rapid adoption (Curley and Salmelin 2013). While the paradigm of open innovation as the concept of circular economy cannot be traced back to one date or author but rather to different schools of thought (Wautelet 2020), legislation creation in the field of open innovation at the EU level officially started in 2013.

In 2013 the European Commission (2013, 4) emphasized that open innovation is a synonym for modern, highly dynamic and interactive processes in the European context. Linear and sequential mindsets are slowly changing to be more opportunistic, more daring and more action-oriented. In the EU, we need to move from having 'perfect plans for yesterday' to an innovation culture that fosters experimentation and prototyping in real-world settings. This innovation culture leads to simultaneous technological and societal innovation and encouragement. We need to be daring and experiment with disruptive approaches as gradual improvement does not correctly reflect the potential of omnipresent, fast-developing information-communication technologies (ICT) for parallel innovations (European Commission 2013).

In 2020 the European Commission launched '*Shaping Europe's Digital Future*' strategy. Over the following five years it was going to focus on three critical digital objectives (European Commission 2022o; Tosdevin 2020):

– technology that works for people;
– a fair and competitive economy;
– an open, democratic, and sustainable society.

'*Shaping Europe's Digital Future*' strategy is one of the priorities under '*A Europe Fit for the Digital Age: Empowering People with a New Generation of Technologies*', which aims to make transformation work for people and businesses while helping to achieve its target of a climate-neutral Europe by 2050 (European Commission 2020a). One of the activities under the mentioned strategy is '*Open Innovation 2.0*' (OI2) as a positive approach to innovation that helps solve critical European challenges by embracing change and not resisting it (European Commission 2020c).

As stated in the political priorities of Commissioner Moedas (European Commission 2015b), creating, and supporting an Open Innovation ecosystem encourages dynamic knowledge circulation and facilitates the translation of that knowledge into socio-economic value. The Commission aims to ensure that the appropriate framework conditions for innovation are in place through the three pillars of its Open Innovation policy: reforming the regulatory environment, boosting private investment and maximizing impacts. Firstly, Europe needs to create the right regulatory environment that removes obstacles to innovation and encourages innovators and entrepreneurs while rules and standard setting must keep up with rapidly changing technologies. Fewer regulatory barriers will help promote more investment in innovation, but much more needs to be done. This brings us to the second pillar: when comparing the levels of investment in the EU and the US it's clear that the European innovation ecosystem lacks adequate private financial instruments. Under the third pillar, the European Commission will strive to get the most out of EU-level support for innovation by developing new actions to bring more innovation impact out of Horizon 2020, including through better synergies with the Structural Funds (European Commission 2015b).

A chronological overview of the key published milestones, which are crucial in the context of the chapter, is given below (European Commission 2022d):

- Revised Europe's ICT Strategy
- Open Innovation and Public Policy in Europe
- Intellectual Property and Legal Issues in Open Innovation in Services
- The Trends of Open Innovation in Services
- Put User in the Centre for Services – A reference model
- Service Innovation Yearbook 2009–2010
- OSI – Socio-Economic Impact of Open Service Innovation – SMART 2009/0077 study
- Service Innovation Yearbook 2010–2011
- Unlocking the Digital Future through Open Innovation – An Intellectual Capital Approach (A critical analysis of open innovation as structural capital)
- Open Innovation 2012
- The Gap – ICT vs. Legal Institutions
- Open Innovation 2.0 Yearbook 2013 – OISPG
- Open Innovation 2.0 – A New Paradigm and Foundation for a Sustainable Europe
- Actions for a Sustainable and Competitive Open Innovation Ecosystem in the EU from a US perspective
- Open Innovation 2.0 Yearbook 2014 – OISPG
- Open Innovation 2.0 Yearbook 2015

– Open Innovation 2.0 Yearbook 2016
– Open Innovation 2.0 yearbook 2017–2018.

Considering that Open Innovation 2.0 has been featured on the European Commission's website for the year 2018 but no announcements were made during the Covid-19 epidemic period, it suggests that the field is still developing.

However, even if announcements and milestones for Open Innovation 2.0 are not directly traceable during the epidemic, this does not mean that activities in this area have not taken place.

As stated by Gabriel (2021), Commissioner for Innovation, Research and Culture, Education and Youth, the European Commission pledged just over €1 billion from Horizon 2020, the EU's Research, and Innovation Program (2014–2020), to tackle the epidemic. So far, €602.3 million has been awarded to support research and innovation projects to tackle many aspects of the epidemic (Gabriel 2021). These projects address the development of diagnostics, treatments, vaccines, epidemiology, preparedness and response to outbreaks, socioeconomics, mental health, production and digital technologies, and the infrastructures and data resources that enable this research. Real-time updates are available on the European Commission's dedicated coronavirus R&I website. It also mobilized €400 million in financing from the Horizon 2020 InnovFin, including InnovFin EFSI and Infectious Diseases Finance Facility, of which €178.5 million has been allocated to accelerate the development of vaccines and other interventions, drugs, medical and diagnostic devices or novel critical research and innovation infrastructures (Gabriel 2021).

8. Conclusions

The European Coalition policy does more than only the steering of the development and distributes finances to two more or less developed regions. It aims to balance development and that also influences the balance of power between national actors. On the other hand, there are indications that long-term effects and long-term partnerships are not taken into the account to the extent they should be. It was proven by researchers that when the financing stops also partnerships cease to exist. What is more concerning is that some of the key results that are being pushed by the European Commission might have negative consequences in future especially those regarding the environment.

The policy 2021 2027 was set even before the evaluation of the previous policy was done, which is a common lifecycle of a policy. Nevertheless, we need to know that the current policy was set with knowledge of current affairs in the geopolitical, social, economic and environmental aspects with a predisposition that no changes would happen shortly. It just came about that each of those aspects has drastically changed in the past few years and has become a major challenge. To be able to tackle that we would need to focus on common goals. There is an issue however how to achieve those goals if we cannot identify with them or if we do not feel the affiliation to them in the manner, we have discussed at the beginning on how we live and see our regions. The same aspect applies to common goals. It is not something that can be only set or determined from top to bottom, but it needs to be something deeper – linked to personal emotions – so we can achieve a collective movement towards the goals. As argued by Crescenzi, Frates and Monastiriotis (2020), an effective and politically sustainable Cohesion Policy needs member states to take (again) full responsibility and ownership and regain a substantive role between Brussels and the regions to ensure the necessary coordination and facilitate regional cooperation (Crescenzi, Fratesi, and Monastiriotis 2020).

Further on, some old ways are still the best ways such as self-sufficiency in food, materials, half products, products and knowledge. Not everything is in profit. There have been cases of moving industries outside of Europe. There have been cases of severe steering of agriculture in a manner of which plants to grow or not to grow, to gain what is more lucrative and what is not. Those policies led to job losses and a lack of certain food sources which now need to be imported and that heavily influenced the environment and the prices of agriculture. Similar cases happened in the industry as well. The real question for the steering of regional development would then be: how do we want to live and what price are we paying for that? Perhaps the OECDs' Better Life Index just might have a partial answer to that question.

Following the argument, one additional notion cannot pass unnoticed – the remark, the EU is not alone in the globalised world and while questioning itself on how to steer the discourse of implementation of the New Industrial Strategy we have to be aware, the world competition does not wait, and the other countries are speeding up in the developmental race. The global changes are occurring at rapid speed, challenges occur on daily basis – from the Russian war on Ukraine and EU struggles due to energetic reliance to Russian gas; towards threatening of potential epidemics – as the world experienced with Covid-19 virus. Worth mentioning is also aging of population and challenges arising from the realities of potential mass migrations. All and all, the world is indeed uncertain and unstable, liquid, as Bauman (2013) describes it. The individuals are becoming also almost liquid personalities transforming from one role to another living in an era post post-truth. The main question therefore persists – is discourse steering in the era of constant change even possible? What are the common values we can relate to and are those values the ones the New Industrial Strategy is addressing? Is the innovation in relation to environmental issues be the solution? Is circularity the solution to the issues related to need for scarce raw materials? Is the new humanism response to the needs of reinforcement of the value chains and new forms of collaboration the New Industrial Industry is desiring to achieve. Can the entrepreneurial state contribute to this shift in values and can we really speak of the values promotion in the late post-modern societies of the European union?

Based on everything said, we have to agree the New Industrial Strategy is making sure the focus of the Europe 2020 is still in sight – the millions of jobs for the Europeans. Additionally, we have to agree the strategy is vast and ambitious and due to its interrelation to numerous initiatives and action plans, the discourse on its implementation and adoption will be difficult to control. However, if strategic approach is used in communication the most opportune way is to tailor the main messages short and understandable: the more competitive globally and more autonomous internally. The two main messages of the EU should be comprehensive and the measures should be simple enough for all EU citizens to understand and request ownership over it. Namely, in the light of global competition with the need to raise labour productivity and international competitiveness (Bartlett 2014), the ambitious New Industrial Strategy seems the proper response. However, the million-dollar question remains: in the swirl of discourses, will it succeed?

The European Innovation Policy was and remained tightly linked to the idea of social development, equality and solution to trending global challenges (e.g., pollution, poverty, etc.) (Lundvall and Borrás 2005; European Union 2019)

Despite its initial aspects of promoting and enhancing innovation potential, it focuses on dealing with important social and political mainstream problems through channelling these innovation actions. As such, it is not only a promoter of competitiveness but also of sustainable growth and democratic development. But a good policy is not solely about formulation. After being implemented, it needs assessment to comprehend its actual value and achievements and develop future perspectives. This raises additional questions about whether the EU innovation assessment tools can cope with these ambitious visions. As such, the chapter took it upon itself to compare the EU Innovation Policy of 2014–2019 with the European Innovation Scoreboard (2014–2021) and assess the degree to which these are compatible. The idea was not to evaluate the policy or the tool and neither to consider the validity of the indicators. The endeavour considers an easy and general approach, answering the question: "Can one see the EU innovation policy reflected in the EIS' summary score?"

The implementation of policy and the development of assessment tools go hand in hand in many aspects, establishing a cohesive view (at least partially) of the regional and national performance of EU members. Only a few parameters (3 out of 38 considered) in the EIS could not be directly linked to the policy agenda, but even those follow the trend set by the strategy. Except for some policy actions targeting the Horizon 2020 applications and policy mechanisms, the indexes can at least indirectly suggest whether the policy achieved its goals. Therefore, the Summary Index can generally suggest whether a member state is following the EU recommendations and the efficiency of its efforts. In this regard, EIS has more parameters concerning the environmental factors (leading to innovation such as Human Resources) and not the outcome of innovation. The question of the validity of these measurements was raised before (Bielińska-Dusza and Hamerska 2021) and is not the main concern of the chapter. Nevertheless, the idea of introducing these parameters leads to the conclusion that EIS can capture the Policy Parameters better than the innovation performance *per se*. This statement should not come as criticism of the Scoreboard's importance in comparing innovative performance across the EU. It is only to suggest that it is attuned to the policy vector of the EU.

One weak aspect of the European Innovation Scoreboard is the fixation on EU-average. The tool is, therefore, best for comparing the national performance of EU members but cannot be used to identify the position of the EU in a wider (global) frame. Adding foreign countries does not solve this issue, as the benchmark is still the EU-28 (now 27) average performance. One thing is clear – the Scoreboard did not follow the EU-Openness in this regard, remaining an in-house comparison tool.

Their close compatibility should not be a striking discovery as if these were randomly correlated. The changes to policy and assessment platforms come gradually. The decision to "Open" European Innovation was not a radical development. Adopting the Open Innovation approach was gradually happening before the 2014 policy. Even earlier formulations acknowledge the importance of cooperating for the common benefit and accessing non-EU skills. Moreover, it is clear in the formulation process as any new Innovation Policy continues the main trends of previous set goals and adds new layers and vectors (see the difference between European Union 2019 and the European Commission 2022a). The same is true for the EIS, continuously upgrading and reshaping the set of indexes as the needs arise. To emphasize the same idea of Openness, the parameter counting the non-EU PhD students is seen in the 2012 Innovation Scoreboard (European Commission 2012b), two years before the 3O's strategy. It only reinforces the idea that the EIS is built to assess the innovation as seen through the Strategic (Formulation) lenses, contributing to the discourse retention (Jessop 2004; 2010).

This comparison leads to one final thought. Maybe we should not see the EU policy and related tools as Pictures in an Album but rather as a Movie. Acknowledging that this is a process and that things drag each other by the hand helps accept the interlinked practices and should affect the way researchers see the policy-evaluation. Furthermore, if a parameter is to emerge on the political horizon, it will inevitably become a part of selection and retention mechanisms.

Having said all the above, we must not forget, the EU has the ambition to be a global leader in the areas of climate change and sustainability. Achieving this objective requires a research and innovation programme that will not only effectively support the sustainability and carbon neutrality path, but will also reinforce the leadership of the EU in technological and social solutions internationally. Policies to green the economy and policies to develop skills should be well connected (Fanello 2012). Following the Covid-19 pandemic and the worsening of climate change, SD is not anymore, an option, but a way all EU MS have to follow to avoid additional natural disasters. In recent decades, the EU has taken steps to straighten its strategies towards limiting the environmental impacts, favouring reduction policies, and ecological productions in various ways, supported by the latest NGEU multiple subsidies. In this context, and EU NRRP probably represents the most concrete support that has been offered so far for the ecological transition in the EU.

On the other hand, business environments built on IS principles, use fewer natural resources than traditional industrial value chains. This makes them more resource efficient and competitive, using less water and energy, and producing less waste and CO2. Enabling more IS also helps the EU meet its global climate change and UN SDG promises.

Regardless of the stated above, if actual EU policies enough support IS development in the EU, could be partly confirmed, since the EU targets to remove all barriers to innovation and the perspective position for innovations, build additional framework conditions for an innovative IS by setting up a IS strategic agenda, harmonised EU regulatory framework and standardisation. As the EU claims, we still need a strong effort of investment similar to the Marshall plan (U.S. program providing aid to Western Europe, following the devastation of World War II.), for the recovery and modernization of Our economy. This means heavily investing in the green transition, transformation, digitalisation, CE and IS in parallel to other policies (European Council 2020).

As also Peter Laybourn, the creator of NISP and Chairman of International Synergies Limited said: "estimate numbers of savings and sales in the EU businesses involving IS, undervalued the "network effect" of increasing power in the industry, encouraging investment and demand-led innovation in a deepening IS ecosystem. Savings on landfill costs alone, show huge potential in all aspects. While combining up diverse sectors/businesses remains complicated, IS could make it worth all the effort" (margaux.legallou 2020). According to the EGD, increasing the IS entails complete responses from each country included in the EU (Núñez Ferrer and Stroia 2020). These should be considered to influence specific goals such as resource efficacy, reducing gas emissions, increasing the exchange in the economy, rising jobs and new businesses. The distribution of enough national estates for "green" encouragements prioritising multinational initiatives and cooperative efforts, to overcome the barriers, are important actions in this view to challenge UN SDG (Stocker 2014; Henriques et al. 2021).

As it was seen, European economies are not bulletproof whether the crisis is an economic or healthcare one. Thus, these crises disrupt the economic development of the European continent. The latest crises, highlighted the weakness of the developed economies, but also reiterated the need to redress the disparities between advanced and emerging economies.

The previous attempt, which aims to address poorer regions by offering them the necessary tools to improve their productivity growth and potential growth, the Cohesion policy, noticed difficulties in achieving its goals. Thus, the European Commission alongside the European Union member states have come up with a plan that is aimed to stimulate the economic growth and continue the previous strategies. The flexibility of the Recovery Plan, lies in its robustness in tackling individual problems of the member states countries. As a result, in the moment individual countries highlighted their strategies in tackling the created disparities, the European Commission pinpointed clear steps, milestones and supervision mechanisms in the implementation of the Plan.

One of key aspects that Romania subscribed under this plan, is increasing the level of innovativeness, thus contributing not only to the innovation development, but also helping Romania in achieving a knowledge-based economy. A number of reforms and investments for the Business Support, Research, Development and Innovation pillar ought to be carried out. Thus, a great emphasize is on the creation of the Excellence Centres and a great emphasize is on recruiting foreign researchers. By doing this, the added value of this approach is not only in creating good conditions for reverse brain drain (meanwhile Romania have severe issues with the aspect of brain drain) and retaining them. Nonetheless, local research institutes, will have the possibility to gain experience from the collaboration with foreign researchers, thus contributing to Romania's R&D.

Lastly, it is important to keep an eye on the implementation of the Recovery Plan, because as mentioned earlier, future financing within the programme, is directly linked to the implementation and achievement of the goals and milestones. This can constitute a great opportunity to launch the Romanian economy to another level – toward a knowledge-based economy, by interconnecting the private sector with the research one, not without a restructure of the later.

Even though we have not come across any research addressing the same issue we are tackling in this chapter, it is certainly worth pointing out the following. Firstly, different stakeholders concur that *New Circular Economy Action Plan* did not cover some areas that should have been investigated to facilitate completion of the plan itself. 'Open Innovation (2.0)' remains one such area as it is a prerequisite for the transition to circular economy and has been proven to be a successful method in many successful examples in the EU. Secondly, Potočnik (2021) agrees that the bare minimum conditions must be provided to effectively coordinate post-Covid-19 and European Green Deal approaches. Without them, EU countries and sectors will face unequal health and economic effects of the Covid-19 epidemic. Strong unity will also prevent further spread of threatening radicalism and its effects which are working to undermine the core EU values and might potentially cause the demise of the EU (Potočnik 2021).

Thirdly, the relationship between research and innovation take-up in Europe has always been in favour of the first. To improve innovation adoption, improved EU policies implement a more universal perspective for research, development and innovation (RD&I). These ambitious policies should encourage more

Europeans to take measured risks and reap the benefits of new higher-expectation businesses (Curley and Salmelin 2013)

Fourthly and as strictly emphasized by Tagliapietra and Veugelers (2020), the green industrial policy needs breakthrough innovation. Public institutions thus need a new perspective on what it means to fail since failure represents a very viable outcome. To encourage cutting edge ideas, recipients must have access to different, yet still sizable, financing sources with diminished administrative requirements. Innovation is risky, therefore grants should be awarded to high-risk ideas which in case of positive outcome promise high returns. For EU green industrial policy to be innovation-driven, it needs to recognize that some projects will not have a positive outcome and to remember that no-risk ideas are rarely the source of innovation in general. The policy should encourage testing of experimental ideas (Tagliapietra and Veugelers 2020).

Finally, the answer to the question based on an argument by Potočnik (2021): *Can the Covid-19 epidemic serve as an opportunity to accelerate the achievement of goals?* Covid-19 has spared no one. It is now clear that a well-coordinated approach globally and, in the EU, could have provided more efficient answers and saved lives. In the future, challenges of a global nature can only be efficiently addressed by joining forces and cooperating. The same is true of the European Green Deal challenges, particularly as they relate to climate change. The only way to address them is by deeper, stronger cooperation, especially in the field of circular economy. We need to see it as the only feasible method of future operation and will need to accept it as part of our everyday life.

Tu sum up, when discussing about sociological, policy, and regional considerations on development and implementation of the EU long-term policies myriad of views and interpretations are possible. However, it remains clear the strong commitment of relevant stakeholders is requested to join forces and claim strategy's ownership to properly implement it. But prior doing so, the realities of post-modern life dictate the strong competition in discourses surrounding the policies and the ones selected and retended. If the retention is continuous also the implementation will be successful and goals achieved.

References

"A European Green Deal." 2022. Text. European Commission - European Commission. Accessed March 23, 2022. https://ec.europa.eu/info/strategy/priorities-2019-2024/european-green-deal_en.

Adelle, Camilla, and Marc Pallemaerts. 2009. "Sustainable Development Indicators–Overview of Relevant FP-Funded Research and Identification of Further Needs." *Europen Comission, Brussels*.

Aiginger, Karl, and Dani Rodrik. 2020. "Rebirth of Industrial Policy and an Agenda for the Twenty-First Century." *Journal of Industry, Competition and Trade* 20 (2): 189–207. https://doi.org/10.1007/s10842-019-00322-3.

Akimova, Liudmyla M., Nataliia L. Khomiuk, Ivan M. Bezena, and Iryna L. Lytvynchuk. 2020. "Planning of Socio-Economic Development of the Territories (Experience of European Union)." *International Journal of Management (IJM)* 11 (4): 567–75.

Alcidi, Cinzia, Sara Baiocco, Francesco Corti, Karel Lannoo, Andrea Renda, Malorie Schaus, and Agnes Sipiczki. 2021. "The New Industrial Strategy for Europe." *Intereconomics* 2021 (3): 132–132.

Audretsch, David B. 2014. "From the Entrepreneurial University to the University for the Entrepreneurial Society." *The Journal of Technology Transfer* 39 (3): 313–21. https://doi.org/10.1007/s10961-012-9288-1.

Ayres, Robert U. 1989. Industrial Metabolism: work in progress. In: van den Bergh, J.C.J.M., Hofkes, M.W. (eds) Theory and Implementation of Economic Models for Sustainable Development. *Economy & Environment* 15. Springer, Dordrecht. https://doi.org/10.1007/978-94-017-3511-7_10

Baas, Leo. 2011. Planning and Uncovering Industrial Symbiosis: Comparing the Rotterdam and Östergötland Regions. *Business Strategy and the Environment* 20 (7): 428–440. https://doi.org/10.1002/bse.735.

Bachtler, John, and Colin Wren. 2006. "Evaluation of European Union Cohesion Policy: Research Questions and Policy Challenges." *Regional Studies* 40 (2): 143–53. https://doi.org/10.1080/00343400600600454.

Bachtrögler, Julia, Ugo Fratesi, and Giovanni Perucca. 2020. "The Influence of the Local Context on the Implementation and Impact of EU Cohesion Policy." *Regional Studies* 54 (1): 21–34. https://doi.org/10.1080/00343404.2018.1551615.

Bartlett, William. 2014. "Shut Out? South East Europe and the EU's New Industrial Policy." SSRN Scholarly Paper 2534513. Rochester, NY: Social Science Research Network. https://doi.org/10.2139/ssrn.2534513.

Bauman, Zygmunt. 2013. *Liquid Modernity*. John Wiley & Sons.

Becker, Sascha O., Peter H. Egger, and Maximilian von Ehrlich. 2018. "Effects of EU Regional Policy: 1989–2013." *Regional Science and Urban Economics* 69 (March): 143–52. https://doi.org/10.1016/j.regsciurbeco.2017.12.001.

Bemelmans-Videc, Marie-Louise, Ray C. Rist, and Evert Vedung. 2017. "Policy Instruments: Typologies and Theories." In *Carrots, Sticks & Sermons*, 21–58. Routledge.

Besednjak Valič, Tamara. 2014. *Oblikovanje Economsko-Socialnega Polja Turističnega Igralništva in Njegovi Vplivi Na Ugodno Razmerje Med Koristmi in Stroški Od Iger Na Srečo (Shaping Economic-Social Field of Turism Gambling and Its Impacts to Favourable Ratios between Benefits and Costs of Gambling)*. Nova Gorica: School of Advanced Social Studies.

Besednjak Valič, Tamara. 2019. "Innovation, Digitalisation, and the HPC in the Danube Region." Edited by Borut Rončević, Coscodaru, Raluca, and Fric, Urška. *Go with the Flow: High Performance Computing and Innovations in the Danube Region*, 22–46.

Besednjak Valič, Tamara. 2022. "Open Innovation and Its Impacts on Interorganisational Stability: A SOFIA Perspective Addressing the Sustainable Growth in Regional Context." In *Technologies and Innovations in Regional Development: The European Union and Its Strategies.*, 80–98.

Besednjak Valič, Tamara, Janez Kolar, and Urša Lamut. 2021. "Fighting the Big Bad Wolf of Global Trends: Technology Transfer between HPC Centres and SMEs." *Digital Policy, Regulation and Governance* ahead-of-print (ahead-of-print). https://doi.org/10.1108/DPRG-11-2020-0162.

Bielińska-Dusza, Edyta, and Monika Hamerska. 2021. "Methodology for Calculating the European Innovation Scoreboard—Proposition for Modification." *Sustainability* 13 (4): 2199. https://doi.org/10.3390/su13042199.

Bigliardi, Barbara, and Francesco Galati. 2016. "Which Factors Hinder the Adoption of Open Innovation in SMEs?" *Technology Analysis & Strategic Management* 28 (8): 869–85. https://doi.org/10.1080/09537325.2016.1180353.

BIN@PORTO. 2018. "Open Innovation Towards Circular Economy." 2018. https://www.eua.eu/news/126:bin-porto-2018-%E2%80%9Copen-innovation-towards-circular-economy%E2%80%9D.html.

Blom-Hansen, Jens. 2005. "Principals, Agents, and the Implementation of EU Cohesion Policy." *Journal of European Public Policy* 12 (4): 624–48. https://doi.org/10.1080/13501760500160136.

Bogers, Marcel, Henry Chesbrough, and Carlos Moedas. 2018. "Open Innovation: Research, Practices, and Policies." *California Management Review* 60 (2): 5–16. https://doi.org/10.1177/0008125617745086.

Borcharhardt, Klaus-Dieter, Jones, Christopher. 2022. "European Commission Introduces REPowerEU: Joint European Action for More Affordable, Secure and Sustainable Energy." Sanctions & Export Controls Update. March 10, 2022. https://sanctionsnews.bakermckenzie.com/european-commission-introduces-repowereu-joint-european-action-for-more-affordable-secure-and-sustainable-energy/.

Borghetto, Enrico, and Fabio Franchino. 2010. "The Role of Subnational Authorities in the Implementation of EU Directives." *Journal of European Public Policy* 17 (6): 759–80. https://doi.org/10.1080/13501763.2010.486972.

Brada, Josef C., Paweł Gajewski, and Ali M. Kutan. 2021. "Economic Resiliency and Recovery, Lessons from the Financial Crisis for the COVID-19 Pandemic: A Regional Perspective from Central and Eastern Europe." *International Review of Financial Analysis* 74. https://doi.org/10.1016/j.irfa.2021.101658.

Braun, Mats. 2016. *Europeanization of Environmental Policy in the New Europe: Beyond Conditionality*. Routledge.

Bruck, Robin. 2016. "A European Vision for Industrial Symbiosis : Recommendations for a Successful European IS Strategy." Info:eu-repo/semantics/bachelorThesis. June 29, 2016. http://essay.utwente.nl/70464/.

Camarinha-Matos, Luis M., Rosanna Fornasiero, Javaneh Ramezani, and Filipa Ferrada. 2019. "Collaborative Networks: A Pillar of Digital Transformation." *Applied Sciences* 9 (24): 5431. https://doi.org/10.3390/app9245431.

Chang, Ha-Joon. 1994. *The Political Economy of Industrial Policy*. 1996th edition. Basingstoke: Palgrave Macmillan.

Chertow, Marian R. 2007. "'Uncovering' Industrial Symbiosis." https://doi.org/10.1162/jiec.2007.1110.

Chertow, Marian R., and D. Rachel Lombardi. 2005. "Quantifying Economic and Environmental Benefits of Co-Located Firms," September. https://doi.org/10.1021/es050050+.

Chesbrough, Henry. 2003. "The Era of Open Innovation." *MITSloan Management Review* 44 (3): 9.

Chesbrough, Henry. 2006. "Open Innovation: A New Paradigm for Understanding Industrial Innovation." In *Chesbrough, H., Vanhaverbeke, W., and West, J., Open Innovation: Researching a New Paradigm.*:1–12.

Chesbrough, Henry, and Adrienne Kardon Crowther. 2006. "Beyond High Tech: Early Adopters of Open Innovation in Other Industries." *R and D Management* 36 (3): 229–36. https://doi.org/10.1111/j.1467-9310.2006.00428.x.

Chesbrough, Henry, and Wim Vanhaverbeke. 2011. "OPEN INNOVATION AND PUBLIC POLICY IN EUROPE." ESADE Business School & the Science I Business Innovation Board AISBL. www.sciencebusiness.net.

Chesbrough, Henry W, and Melissa M Appleyard. 2007. "Open Innovation and Strategy." 50 (1): 21.

Chun, Yoon-Young, and Kun-Mo Lee. 2017. "Environmental Impacts of the Rental Business Model Compared to the Conventional Business Model: A Korean Case of Water Purifier for Home Use." *The International Journal of Life Cycle Assessment* 22 (7): 1096–1108. https://doi.org/10.1007/s11367-016-1227-1.

Cimoli, Mario, Giovanni Dosi, and Joseph E. Stiglitz, eds. 2009. *Industrial Policy and Development: The Political Economy of Capabilities Accumulation*. Initiative for Policy Dialogue. Oxford: Oxford University Press. https://doi.org/10.1093/acprof:oso/9780199235261.001.0001.

CircLean. 2022. "Industrial Symbiosis in the EU Policy Landscape." News. *Industrial Symbiosis in the EU Policy Landscape* (blog). 2022. https://circlean-symbiosis.eu/new/industrial-symbiosis-in-the-eu-policy-landscape/.

COM. 2020. "102 Final: A New Industrial Strategy for Europe." EU Comission. https://ec.europa.eu/info/sites/default/files/communication-eu-industrial-strategy-march-2020_en.pdf.

———. 2021. "350 Final: Updating the 2020 New Industrial Strategy: Building a Stronger Single Market for Europe's Recovery." EU Comission. https://ec.europa.eu/info/sites/default/files/communication-industrial-strategy-update-2020_en.pdf.

Costa, Inês, and Paulo Ferrão. 2010. "A Case Study of Industrial Symbiosis Development Using a Middle-out Approach." *Journal of Cleaner Production* 18 (10): 984–92. https://doi.org/10.1016/j.jclepro.2010.03.007.

Costa, Inês, Guillaume Massard, and Abhishek Agarwal. 2010. "Waste Management Policies for Industrial Symbiosis Development: Case Studies in European Countries."

Crescenzi, Riccardo, Ugo Fratesi, and Vassilis Monastiriotis. 2020. "Back to the Member States? Cohesion Policy and the National Challenges to the European Union." *Regional Studies* 54 (1): 5–9. https://doi.org/10.1080/00343404.2019.1662895.

Crescenzi, Riccardo, and Mara Giua. 2020. "One or Many Cohesion Policies of the European Union? On the Differential Economic Impacts of Cohesion Policy across Member States." *Regional Studies* 54 (1): 10–20. https://doi.org/10.1080/00343404.2019.1665174.

Curley, Martin, and Bro Salmelin. 2013. "Open Innovation 2.0: A New Paradigm." *OI2 Conference Paper*. https://uc-dk.dk/uasnet/wp-content/uploads/Open-Innovation-2.0-Salmelin.pdf.

Daddi, Tiberio, Benedetta Nucci, and Fabio Iraldo. 2017. "Using Life Cycle Assessment (LCA) to Measure the Environmental Benefits of Industrial

Symbiosis in an Industrial Cluster of SMEs." *Journal of Cleaner Production* 147: 157–64. https://doi.org/10.1016/J.JCLEPRO.2017.01.090.

Dahlander, Linus, and David M. Gann. 2010. "How Open Is Innovation?" *Research Policy* 39: 699–709.

Deutz, Pauline. 2014. "Food for Thought: Seeking the Essence of Industrial Symbiosis." In . Springer. https://doi.org/10.1007/978-3-319-03826-1_1.

Directorate-General for Budget (European Commission). 2021. *The EU's 2021-2027 Long-Term Budget and NextGenerationEU: Facts and Figures.* LU: Publications Office of the European Union. https://data.europa.eu/doi/10.2761/808559.

Džajić Uršič, E. 2020a. "Systematized Analysis Using Data Mining's Methodology on the Topic of Regional Industrial Symbiosis and Its Networks." *Research in Social Change*, 2020. https://www.fuds.si/wp-content/uploads/2020/11/RSC_Volume_12_Issue_3_2020_Dzajic-Ursic_78-99.pdf.

Džajić Uršič, E.. 2020b. "Morphogenesis of Industrial Symbiotic Networks." Berlin: Peter Lang. doi 10 (2020): b16330

Eckert, Eva, and Oleksandra Kovalevska. 2021. "Sustainability in the European Union: Analyzing the Discourse of the European Green Deal." *Journal of Risk and Financial Management* 14 (2): 80. https://doi.org/10.3390/jrfm14020080.

Ehrenfeld, John, and Nicholas Gertler. 1997. "Industrial Ecology in Practice: The Evolution of Interdependence at Kalundborg." https://doi.org/10.1162/jiec.1997.1.1.67.

Eilering, Janet AM, and Walter JV Vermeulen. 2004. "Eco-Industrial Parks: Toward Industrial Symbiosis and Utility Sharing in Practice." https://scholar.google.si/scholar?q=Eco-industrial+parks:+Toward+industrial+symbiosis+and+utility+sharing+in+practice&hl=en&as_sdt=0&as_vis=1&oi=scholart#:~:text=%5BPDF%5D%20researchgate.net.

Ellen MacArthur Foundation. 2019. "Circular Economy Introduction." 2019. https://ellenmacarthurfoundation.org/topics/circular-economy-introduction/overview.

Ellen MacArthur Foundation. 2020. "Concept. What Is a Circular Economy? A Framework an Economy That Is Restorative and Regenerative by Design." 2020. https://www.ellenmacarthurfoundation.org/circular-economy/concept.

Enkel, Ellen, Oliver Gassmann, and Henry Chesbrough. 2009. "Open R&D and Open Innovation: Exploring the Phenomenon." *R&D Management* 39 (4): 311–16. https://doi.org/10.1111/j.1467-9310.2009.00570.x.

Erman. 2020. "Prospects for Innovation Performance on European Level." *Research in Social Change* 12 (3): 100–114. https://doi.org/10.2478/rsc-2020-0016.

EU Cohesion Policy implementation in Slovenia. 2020. "Recovery and Resilience Plan." Recovery and Resilience Plan. 2020. https://www.eu-skladi.si/en/post-2020-1/recovery-and-resilience-plan.

EU Monitor. 2022. "Circular Economy: Definition, Importance, and Benefits." 2022. https://www.eumonitor.eu/9353000/1/j9vvik7m1c3gyxp/vknegugz7hwu?ctx=vjxzjv7ta8z.

EURIS. 2012. "Embracing Open Innovation in Europe." https://wrs.region-stuttgart.de/uploads/media/publikationen_euris_guide.pdf.

European Commission. 2001. "SEC(2001) 1414 2001 Innovation Scoreboard."

European Commission. 2006. "COM(2006) 502 Final. Putting Knowledge into Practice: A Broad-Based Innovation Strategy for the EU."

European Commission. 2010. "Europe 2020. A Strategy for Smart, Sustainable and Inclusive Growth."

European Commission. 2012a. "COM/2012/060 Final. Innovating for Sustainable Growth: A Bioeconomy for Europe." https://eur-lex.europa.eu/legal-content/EN/TXT/?uri=CELEX%3A52012DC0060.

European Commission. 2012b. *Regional Innovation Scoreboard 2012*. LU: Publications Office. https://data.europa.eu/doi/10.2769/55659.

European Commission. 2013. "Open Innovation 2.0. Open Innovation." 2013. https://www.urenio.org/wp-content/uploads/2008/11/2013-Open-Innovation-Yearbook-2013.pdf.

European Commission. 2014. "Research and Innovation." Text. POLICY Research and Innovation. 2014. https://ec.europa.eu/info/strategy/research-and-innovation_en.

European Commission. 2015a. "COM/2015/0614. Closing the Loop - An EU Action Plan for the Circular Economy." https://eur-lex.europa.eu/legal-content/EN/TXT/?uri=CELEX%3A52015DC0614.

European Commission. 2015b. "Open Innovation, Open Science, Open to the World – a Vision for the Europe." 2015. https://op.europa.eu/en/publication-detail/-/publication/3213b335-1cbc-11e6-ba9a-01aa75ed71a1.

European Commission. 2015c. "Industrial Symbiosis: Realising the Circular Economy." Text. Eco-Innovation Action Plan - European Commission. July 14, 2015. https://ec.europa.eu/environment/ecoap/about-eco-innovation/experts-interviews/20140127_industrial-symbiosis-realising-the-circular-economy_en.

European Commission. 2015d. "Sustainable Development Goals and the Agenda2030." Text. Sustainable Development Goals and the Agenda2030. September 25, 2015. https://ec.europa.eu/commission/presscorner/detail/en/MEMO_15_5709.

European Commission. 2016. "Directorate-General for Research and Innovation." H2020 Programme Guidelines on FAIR Data Management in Horizon 2020. 2016. https://ec.europa.eu/research/participants/data/ref/h2020/grants_manual/hi/oa_pilot/h2020-hi-oa-data-mgt_en.pdf.

European Commission. 2018a. "COM/2018/097 Final. Action Plan: Financing Sustainable Growth." https://eur-lex.europa.eu/legal-content/EN/TXT/?uri=CELEX%3A52018DC0097.

European Commission. 2018b. "COM/2018/673 Final. A Sustainable Bioeconomy for Europe: Strengthening the Connection between Economy, Society and the Environment." https://eur-lex.europa.eu/legal-content/EN/TXT/?uri=CELEX%3A52018DC0673.

European Commission. 2018c. "COM/2018/773 Final. Clean Planet for All. A European Strategic Long-Term Vision for a Prosperous, Modern, Competitive and Climate Neutral Economy." https://eur-lex.europa.eu/legal-content/EN/TXT/?uri=CELEX%3A52018DC0773.

European Commission. 2018d. "Measuring progress towards circular economy in the SWD/2018/017 final." https://eur-lex.europa.eu/legal-content/LV/ALL/?uri=CELEX:52018SC0017.

European Commission. 2019a. "COM/2019/640 Final. The European Green Deal." https://eur-lex.europa.eu/legal-content/EN/TXT/?uri=COM%3A2019%3A640%3AFIN.

European Commission. 2019b. *Guide to the Approximation of European Union Environmental Legislation. Part 1: Introduction to the Approximation of Environmental Legislation.* https://ec.europa.eu/environment/archives/guide/part1.htm.

European Commission. 2019c. "Report from the Commission to the European Parliament, the Council, the European Economic and Social Committee and the Committee of the Regions on the Implementation of the Circular Economy Action Plan." https://eur-lex.europa.eu/legal-content/EN/TXT/HTML/?uri=CELEX:52019DC0190&from=fi.

European Commission. 2020a. "Changing How We Produce and Consume: New Circular Economy Action Plan Shows the Way to a Climate-Neutral, Competitive Economy and Empowered Consumers." 2020. https://ec.europa.eu/commission/presscorner/detail/en/ip_20_420.

European Commission. 2020b. "COM/2020/22 Final. Proposal for a REGULATION OF THE EUROPEAN PARLIAMENT AND OF THE COUNCIL Establishing the Just Transition Fund." https://eur-lex.europa.eu/legal-content/EN/TXT/?uri=CELEX%3A52020PC0022.

European Commission. 2020c. "COM/2020/102 Final. A New Industrial Strategy for Europe." https://eur-lex.europa.eu/legal-content/EN/TXT/?uri=CELEX%3A52020DC0102.

European Commission. 2020d. "COM/2020/380 Final. EU Biodiversity Strategy for 2030 Bringing Nature Back into Our Lives." https://eur-lex.europa.eu/legal-content/EN/TXT/?uri=CELEX:52020DC0380.

European Commission. 2020e. "Research and Innovation Analysis in the European Semester 2020 Country Reports." https://ec.europa.eu/info/sites/default/files/research_and_innovation/strategy_on_research_and_innovation/documents/2020_compilation_research_and_innovation_sections_in_country_reports.pdf.

European Commission. 2021a. "2030 Climate & Energy Framework." 2021. https://ec.europa.eu/clima/eu-action/climate-strategies-targets/2030-climate-energy-framework_en.

European Commission. 2021b. "European Innovation Scoreboard 2021 Methodology Report.Pdf."

European Commission. 2021c. "Proposal for a Council Implementing Decision on the approval of the assessment of the recovery and resilience plan for Romania." https://ec.europa.eu/info/sites/default/files/com2021_608_annex_en_0.pdf.

European Commission. 2021d. "Recovery Plan." https://ec.europa.eu/info/strategy/recovery-plan-europe_en.

European Commission. 2021e. *Regional Innovation Scoreboard 2021*. European Commission.

European Commission. 2021f. "Regional Innovation Scoreboard 2021 - Methodology Report.Pdf."

European Commission. 2021g. "Summary of the Commission's Assessment of the Romanian Recovery and Resilience Plan." https://ec.europa.eu/info/sites/default/files/ro_rrp_summary.pdf.

European Commission. 2022a. "2050 Long-Term Strategy." 2022. https://ec.europa.eu/clima/eu-action/climate-strategies-targets/2050-long-term-strategy_en.

European Commission. 2022b. "A European Green Deal." Text. A European Green Deal. 2022. https://ec.europa.eu/info/strategy/priorities-2019-2024/european-green-deal_en.

European Commission. 2022c. "After the New Normal: Scenarios for Europe in the Post Covid-19 World." 2022. https://op.europa.eu/en/web/eu-law-and-publications/publication-detail/-/publication/fcb24683-b3bf-11ec-9d96-01aa75ed71a1.

European Commission. 2022d. "Circular Economy Action Plan." 2022. https://environment.ec.europa.eu/strategy/circular-economy-action-plan_en#timeline.

European Commission. 2022e. "Cohesion Policy 2021–2027." 2022. https://ec.europa.eu/regional_policy/en/2021_2027/.

European Commission. 2022f. "COM(2022) 332 Final. A New European Innovation Agenda."

European Commission. 2022g. "COM/2022/230 Final. REPowerEU Plan." https://eur-lex.europa.eu/legal-content/EN/TXT/?uri=COM%3A2022%3A230%3AFIN.

European Commission. 2022h. "From 6 to 27 Members." 2022. https://ec.europa.eu/neighbourhood-enlargement/enlargement-policy/6-27-members_en.

European Commission. 2022i. "History of the Policy." 2022. https://ec.europa.eu/regional_policy/en/policy/what/history/.

European Commission. 2022j. "Priorities for 2014–2020." 2022. https://ec.europa.eu/regional_policy/en/policy/how/priorities/2014-2020/.

European Commission. 2022k. "Priorities for 2021–2027." 2022. https://ec.europa.eu/regional_policy/en/policy/how/priorities.

European Commission. 2022l. "Programming and Implementation." 2022. https://ec.europa.eu/regional_policy/en/policy/how/stages-step-by-step/.

European Commission. 2022m. "Recovery Plan for Europe." Text. 2022. https://ec.europa.eu/info/strategy/recovery-plan-europe_en.

European Commission. 2022n. "The EU's Main Investment Policy." 2022. https://ec.europa.eu/regional_policy/en/policy/what/investment-policy/.

European Commission. 2022o. "The Open Innovation Publications." 2022. https://digital-strategy.ec.europa.eu/en/library/open-innovation-publications.

European Commission. 2022p. "Joint European Action for More Affordable, Secure Energy." Text. *European Commission - European Commission* (blog). March 8, 2022. https://ec.europa.eu/commission/presscorner/detail/en/IP_22_1511.

European Commission. Directorate General for Regional and Urban Policy, SWECO, and t33. 2018. *Development of a System of Common Indicators for European Regional Development Fund and Cohesion Fund Interventions after 2020.Part I, p Thematic Objective 1, 3, 4, 5, 6*. LU: Publications Office. https://data.europa.eu/doi/10.2776/279688.

European Council. 2020. "Videoconferenza dei membri del Consiglio europeo, 23 aprile 2020." 2020. https://www.consilium.europa.eu/it/meetings/european-council/2020/04/23/.

"European Innovation Scoreboard." 2021. https://ec.europa.eu/docsroom/documents/46013.

European Parliament. 2000. "Lisbon European Council 23–24.03.2000: Conclusions of the Presidency." 2000. https://www.europarl.europa.eu/summits/lis1_en.htm.

European Parliament. 2016. *EU Innovation Policy: Part I: Building the EU Innovation Policy Mix, in Depth Analysis.* LU: Publications Office. https://data.europa.eu/doi/10.2861/996440.

European Parliament. 2018. "PE/48/2018/REV/1. Directive (EU) 2018/2001 of the European Parliament and of the Council of 11 December 2018 on the Promotion of the Use of Energy from Renewable Sources (Text with EEA Relevance.)." http://data.europa.eu/eli/dir/2018/2001/oj/eng.

European Parliament, and European Council. 2015. "EU 2015/757. Regulation Of 29 April 2015 on the Monitoring, Reporting and Verification of Carbon Dioxide Emissions from Maritime Transport, and Amending Directive 2009/16/EC." https://eur-lex.europa.eu/eli/reg/2015/757/oj.

European Union. 2014. "Innovation Union Scoreboard 2014," 100.

European Union. 2017. *European Innovation Scoreboard 2017.*

European Union. 2019. *Open Europe: Policies, Reforms and Achievements in EU Science and Innovation 2014–2019.*

European Union. 2022a. "History of the EU." 2022. https://european-union.europa.eu/principles-countries-history/history-eu_en.

European Union. 2022b. "The European Commission's Priorities." Text. European Commission - European Commission. 2022. https://ec.europa.eu/info/strategy/priorities-2019-2024_en.

European Union. 2022c. "European Innovation Scoreboard." Text. European Commission - European Commission. Accessed July 26, 2022. https://ec.europa.eu/info/research-and-innovation/statistics/performance-indicators/european-innovation-scoreboard_en.

EUROSTAT. 2022a. "Data on Employment by Industry." 2022. https://appsso.eurostat.ec.europa.eu/nui/show.do?dataset=nama_10_a10_e&lang=en.

EUROSTAT. 2022b. "GDP per Capita." 2022. https://ec.europa.eu/eurostat/databrowser/view/NAMA_10_PC__custom_2755257/default/table?lang=en.

EUROSTAT. 2022c. "Gross Value Added and Income." 2022. https://appsso.eurostat.ec.europa.eu/nui/show.do?dataset=namq_10_a10&lang=en.

Eurostat. 2022. "Statistics | Eurostat." 2022. https://ec.europa.eu/eurostat/databrowser/view/NAMA_10_PC__custom_3012430/default/table?lang=en.

EY Global. 2022. "European Commission Proposes Package of Measures Announced in Circular Economy Action Plan | Sustainable Products to Be the New Mainstream in the EU." 2022. https://www.ey.com/en_gl/tax-alerts/european-commission-proposes-package-of-measures-announced-in-ceap-sustainable-products-to-be-the-new-mainstream-in-the-eu.

Fanello, Marco. 2012. *Economia Circolare e Agro-Alimentare*, BA Thesis. Università Ca' Foscari Venezia. http://hdl.handle.net/10579/19745.

Fiaschi, Davide, Andrea Mario Lavezzi, and Angela Parenti. 2018. "Does EU Cohesion Policy Work? Theory and Evidence." *Journal of Regional Science* 58 (2): 386–423. https://doi.org/10.1111/jors.12364.

Freire, Clovis. 2013. "Strategies for Structural Transformation in South Asian Countries." SSRN Scholarly Paper 2318330. Rochester, NY: Social Science Research Network. https://papers.ssrn.com/abstract=2318330.

Fric, U. 2019. "Impact of circular economy as the EU's ambitious policy." *Research in Social Change* 11 (2): 79–96. https://doi.org/10.2478/rsc-2019-0010.

Fric, U. 2022. "Is Open Innovation (2.0) Leading to the Circular Economy (2.0)." In *Technologies and Innovations in Regional Development: The European Union and Its Strategies.*, 80–98.

Gabriel, Mariya. 2021. "EU Research and Innovation in Action against the Coronavirus: Funding, Results and Impact." 2021. https://ec.europa.eu/info/sites/default/files/research_and_innovation/research_by_area/documents/ec_rtd_eu-research-innovation-against-covid.pdf.

Gangaliuc, Cristian. 2022. "Clusters vs Networks: A Dilemma for Regional Innovation Policy." In *Technologies and Innovations in Regional Development: The European Union and Its Strategies*, 49–75. Peter Lang Ltd.

Gavril, Ioana Andrada, and Tamara Nae. 2019. "The Perspectives of the European Cohesion Policy for Romania." *Economic Convergence in European Union*, 287.

Gingrich, Caleb. 2012. "Industrial Symbiosis: Current Understandings and Needed Ecology and Economics Influences." https://www.semanticscholar.org/paper/IndustrIal-symbIosIs%3A-Current-understandIngs-and-Gingrich/cbb35fa904de20a1c6f713fe64a41291b806da96.

González-Val, Rafael, and Fernando Pueyo. 2019. "Natural Resources, Economic Growth and Geography." *Economic Modelling* 83: 150–59. https://doi.org/10.1016/j.econmod.2019.02.007.

Greenwald, B, and J E Stiglitz. 2013. "Industrial Policies, the Creation of a Learning Society, and Economic Development," Paper presented to the International Economic Association/World Bank Industrial Policy Roundtable in Washington, DC, May 22–23, 201,, 40.

GROW.DDG1.C.4. 2016. "EU Construction and Demolition Waste Management Protocol." September 30, 2016. https://ec.europa.eu/docsroom/documents/20509/.

Guasti, Petra. 2020. "The Impact of the Covid-19 Pandemic in Central and Eastern Europe the Rise of Autocracy and Democratic Resilience." *Democratic Theory* 7 (2): 47–60. https://doi.org/10.3167/DT.2020.070207.

Hafner, Ana, and Dolores Modic. 2020. "European Automotive Technological Innovation Systems in the Age of Disruption: The Suppliers' View." *Research in Social Change* 12 (3): 53–77. https://doi.org/10.2478/rsc-2020-0014.

Hák, Tomás, Bedrich Moldan, and Arthur Lyon Dahl. 2012. *Sustainability Indicators: A Scientific Assessment*. Vol. 67. Island Press. https://wedocs.unep.org/20.500.11822/30299.

Hartard, Sussane. 2008. "Industrial Ecology and Industrial Symbiosis: New Concepts or New Branding." *Trier: Trier University of Applied Sciences—Umwelt-Campus Birkenfeld, Available Online: Http://Www.up.Edu.Br/Cmspositivo/Uploads/Imagens/Files/Mestrado%20Gest%C3%A3o%20Ambiental/Summer%20school/Hartard.*https://search.iczhiku.com/paper/QMlG9lle5GaBi2K7.pdf.

Hausmann, Ricardo, and Dani Rodrik. 2003. "Economic Development as Self-Discovery." *Journal of Development Economics*, 14th Inter-American Seminar on Economics, 72 (2): 603–33. https://doi.org/10.1016/S0304-3878(03)00124-X.

Haverland, Markus, and Marleen Romeijn. 2007. "Do Member States Make European Policies Work? Analysing the EU Transposition Deficit." *Public Administration* 85 (3): 757–78. https://doi.org/10.1111/j.1467-9299.2007.00670.x.

Henriques, Juan Diego, João Azevedo, Rui Dias, Marco Estrela, Cristina Ascenço, Doroteya Vladimirova, and Karen Miller. 2021. "Implementing Industrial Symbiosis Incentives: An Applied Assessment Framework for Risk Mitigation." *Circular Economy and Sustainability*, June. https://doi.org/10.1007/s43615-021-00069-2.

Herstad, Sverre J, Carter Bloch, Bernd Ebersberger, and Els van de Velde. 2010. "National Innovation Policy and Global Open Innovation: Exploring Balances, Tradeoffs and Complementarities." *Science and Public Policy* 37 (2): 113–24. https://doi.org/10.3152/030234210X489590.

Herva, Marta, Amaya Franco, Eugenio F. Carrasco, and Enrique Roca. 2011. "Review of Corporate Environmental Indicators." *Journal of Cleaner Production* 19 (15): 1687–99. https://doi.org/10.1016/j.jclepro.2011.05.019.

Heymann, Eric, and Stefan Vetter. 2013. "Europe's Re-Industrialisation: The Gulf between Aspiration and Reality," 23.

Howard-Grenville, Jennifer, and Raymond Paquin. 2008. "Organizational Dynamics in Industrial Ecosystems: Insights from Organizational Theory." https://www.researchgate.net/publication/260335548_Organizational_dynamics_in_industrial_ecosystems_Insights_from_organizational_theory.

Jessop, Bob. 2004. "Critical Semiotic Analysis and Cultural Political Economy." *Critical Discourse Studies* 1 (2): 159–74. https://doi.org/10.1080/17405900410001674506.

Jessop, Bob. 2010. "Cultural Political Economy and Critical Policy Studies." *Critical Policy Studies* 3 (3–4): 336–56. https://doi.org/10.1080/19460171003619741.

Jessop, Bob, and Stijn Oosterlynck. 2008. "Cultural Political Economy: On Making the Cultural Turn without Falling into Soft Economic Sociology." *Geoforum* 39 (3): 1155–69. https://doi.org/10.1016/j.geoforum.2006.12.008.

Jesus, Gessica Mina Kim, and Daniel Jugend. 2021. "How Can Open Innovation Contribute to Circular Economy Adoption? Insights from a Literature Review." *European Journal of Innovation Management.*, 2021. https://doi.org/10.1108/EJIM-01-2021-0022.

Joyce, Alexandre, and Raymond L Paquin. 2016. "The Triple Layered Business Model Canvas: A Tool to Design More Sustainable Business Models." *Journal of Cleaner Production* 135: 1474–86.

Kasprzyk, Beata, and Jolanta Wojnar. 2021. "An Evaluation of the Implementation of the Europe 2020 Strategy." *Economic and Regional Studies/Studia Ekonomiczne i Regionalne* 14 (2): 146–57.

Kettunen, M., C. Boywer, L. Vaculova, and C. Charveriat. 2018. "Sustainable Development Goals and the EU: Uncovering the Nexus between External and Internal Policies." *Institute of European Environmental Policy*. https://ieep.eu/uploads/articles/attachments/8399886b-8e29-43f7-b98c-4a714a0f0cc8/t2030-ieep_sdg_globaldimension_final-1.pdf?v=63711750136.

Kleindienst, Petra. 2019. "Economic and Social Security in EU: Reforming Slovenian Law on Social Enterpreneurship." *Research in Social Change* 11 (2): 14–34. https://doi.org/10.2478/rsc-2019-0007.

Koundouri, Phoebe, Stathis Devves, and Angelos Plataniotis. 2021. "Alignment of the European Green Deal, the Sustainable Development Goals and the European Semester Process: Method and Application." *Theoretical Economics Letters* 11 (4): 743–70. https://doi.org/10.4236/tel.2021.114049.

Kurrer, Christian. 2021. "Environment Policy: General Principles and Basic Framework." 2021. https://www.europarl.europa.eu/factsheets/en/sheet/71/environment-policy-general-principles-and-basic-framework.

Laursen, Keld, and Ammon Salter. 2006. "Open for Innovation: The Role of Openness in Explaining Innovation Performance among U.K. Manufacturing Firms." *Strategic Management Journal* 27 (2): 131–50. https://doi.org/10.1002/smj.507.

Lee, Keun. 2013a. "Capability Failure and Industrial Policy to Move beyond the Middle-Income Trap: From Trade-Based to Technology-Based Specialization."

In *The Industrial Policy Revolution I: The Role of Government Beyond Ideology*, edited by Joseph E. Stiglitz and Justin Yifu Lin, 244–72. International Economic Association Series. London: Palgrave Macmillan UK. https://doi.org/10.1057/9781137335173_16.

Lee, Keun. 2013b. *Schumpeterian Analysis of Economic Catch-up: Knowledge, Path-Creation, and the Middle-Income Trap*. Cambridge: Cambridge University Press. https://doi.org/10.1017/CBO9781107337244.

Leonardi, Robert. 2006. "Cohesion in the European Union." *Regional Studies* 40 (2): 155–66. https://doi.org/10.1080/00343400600600462.

Ljubotina. 2021. "The Influence of Entrepreneurial Skills, Education and Risk Perception on Career Choice Intent: The Case of European Students with Family Business Background." *Research in Social Change* 12 (1): 23–37. https://doi.org/10.2478/rsc-2020-0002.

Lucian, Paul. 2015. "From The Lisbon Strategy To Europe 2020." *Studies in Business and Economics* 10 (2): 53–61. https://doi.org/10.1515/sbe-2015-0020.

Lundvall, Bengt-Åke, and Susana Borrás. 2005. "Science, Technology, and Innovation Policy." In *Innovation Handbook*, Fagerberg Jan, Mowery David C. and Nelson Richard R., 599–631. Oxford University Press, Oxford. https://doi.org/10.1093/oxfordhb/9780199286805.003.0022.

MacArthur, Ellen. 2013. "Towards the Circular Economy." *Journal of Industrial Ecology* 2 (1): 23–44. https://www.werktrends.nl/app/uploads/2015/06/Rapport_McKinsey-Towards_A_Circular_Economy.pdf.

Makarovič, Matej, Janez Šušteršič, and Borut Rončević. 2014. "Is Europe 2020 Set to Fail? The Cultural Political Economy of the EU Grand Strategies." *European Planning Studies* 22 (3): 610–26. https://doi.org/10.1080/09654313.2013.782387.

margaux.legallou. 2020. "Eco-Innovation at the Heart of European Policies. Making Industrial Symbiosis 'Business as Usual' for Europe's Circular Economy." Text. Eco-Innovation Action Plan - European Commission. March 30, 2020. https://ec.europa.eu/environment/ecoap/about-eco-innovation/experts-interviews/making-industrial-symbiosis-business-usual-europes-circular_en.

Mazzucato, Mariana, Rainer Kattel, and Josh Ryan-Collins. 2020. "Challenge-Driven Innovation Policy: Towards a New Policy Toolkit." *Journal of Industry, Competition and Trade* 20 (2): 421–37. https://doi.org/10.1007/s10842-019-00329-w.

Mihailovici, Gabriela. 2020. "Financing The Recovery Of The Eu Member States Economies And Implications For Romania In The New Pandemic Context." *Euroinfo* 4 (3): 14–40.

Miotto, Riccardo. 2021. "Eco-Parco Industriale e Sviluppo Sostenibile Nel Solco Delle Strategie Europee e Nazionali per Il Rilancio Dell'economia

Meridionale: Smart Utility District (SUD): Il Progetto Di Riconversione Del Sito Ex Fiat Di Termini Imerese in Un Eco-Parco Industriale. Bachelor's Degree Thesis." https://tesi.luiss.it/id/eprint/31842.

Morikawa, Merit. 2016. "What Is Open Innovation 2.0 and Why Does It Matter?" 2016. https://www.viima.com/blog/what-is-open-innovation-2.0-and-why-does-it-matter.

Ness, Barry, Evelin Urbel-Piirsalu, Stefan Anderberg, and Lennart Olsson. 2007. "Categorising Tools for Sustainability Assessment." *Ecological Economics* 60 (3): 498–508. https://doi.org/10.1016/j.ecolecon.2006.07.023.

Núñez Ferrer, Jorge, and Cristian Stroia. 2020. "An Innovation Policy to Meet the EU's Green Deal Circular Economy Goals. CEPS Policy Insights 25 Sep 2020. [Policy Paper]." http://aei.pitt.edu/103352/.

OECD. 2021. "COVID-19 Recovery Dashboard." OECD. 2021. https://www.oecd.org/coronavirus/en/recovery-dashboard.

OECD. 2022a. "OECD Better Life Index." 2022. https://www.oecdbetterlifeindex.org/.

OECD. 2022b. "Regional Development Policy - OECD." 2022. https://www.oecd.org/regional/regional-policy/regionaldevelopment.htm.

Opiłowska, Elżbieta. 2021. "The Covid-19 Crisis: The End of a Borderless Europe?" *European Societies* 23 (S1): 589–600. https://doi.org/10.1080/14616696.2020.1833065.

Pandiloska Jurak, Alenka. 2019. "Public Policy Instrument Evaluation in Service of Enabling Grand Strategy Discourse – Case of Horizon 2020 Key Indicators." *Research in Social Change* 11 (2): 97–121. https://doi.org/10.2478/rsc-2019-0011.

Pandiloska Jurak, Alenka. 2020. "The Importance of High – Tech Companies for EU Economy – Overview and the EU Grand Strategies Perspective." *Research in Social Change* 12 (3): 32–52. https://doi.org/10.2478/rsc-2020-0013.

Pandiloska Jurak, Alenka. 2021. "Technologies, Innovation & Regional Policy – It Is Not All about Business." Edited by Victor Rončević, Borut, Cepoi Victor. *Technologies and Innovations in Regional Development: The European Union and Its Strategies*, 119–38.

Pandiloska, Jurak, Alenka, and Uroš Pinteric. 2012. "Assessment of Municipalities' Performances in Slovenia." *Transylvanian Review of Administrative Sciences* 2012 (35): 121–37.

Papa, Armando, Roberto Chierici, Luca Vincenzo Ballestra, Dirk Meissner, and Mehmet A. Orhan. 2021. "Harvesting Reflective Knowledge Exchange for Inbound Open Innovation in Complex Collaborative Networks: An Empirical Verification in Europe." *Journal of Knowledge Management* 25 (4): 669–92. https://doi.org/10.1108/JKM-04-2020-0300.

Phillips, Paul S., Richard Barnes, Margaret P. Bates, and Thomas Coskeran. 2006. "A Critical Appraisal of an UK County Waste Minimisation Programme: The Requirement for Regional Facilitated Development of Industrial Symbiosis/Ecology." https://doi.org/10.1016/j.resconrec.2005.07.004.

Pianta, Mario. 2014. "An Industrial Policy for Europe." SSRN Scholarly Paper 2530344. Rochester, NY: Social Science Research Network. https://papers.ssrn.com/abstract=2530344.

Podmenik, Darka, and Maruša Gorišek. 2020. "Is Youth Unemployment in EU Countries Structural?" *Research in Social Change* 12 (2): 80–105. https://doi.org/10.2478/rsc-2020-0010.

Potočnik, Janez. 2021. "The European Green Deal and a Post Covid-19 Prosperity." Ellen MacArthur Foundation. 2021. https://ellenmacarthurfoundation.org/articles/the-european-green-deal-and-a-post-covid-19-prosperity.

Renner, George T. 1947. "Geography of industrial localization." *Economic Geography* 23 (3): 167–189. https://doi.org/10.2307/141510.

Roca, Laurence Clément, and Cory Searcy. 2012. "An Analysis of Indicators Disclosed in Corporate Sustainability Reports." *Journal of Cleaner Production* 20 (1): 103–18. https://doi.org/10.1016/j.jclepro.2011.08.002.

Rodrik, Dani. 2008. "Normalizing Industrial Policy." Working Paper. Washington, DC: World Bank. https://openknowledge.worldbank.org/handle/10986/28009.

Rončević, Borut. 2019. "Cultural Political Economy of Europe 2020 : Jean Monnet Chair CPE 2020 and Its Impact." *Research in Social Change* 11 (2): 5–13.

Rončević, Borut, and Tamara Besednjak Valič. 2022. *An Active Society in a Networked World: The Cultural Political Economy of Grand Strategies*. Berlin, Germany: Peter Lang. https://www.peterlang.com/document/1272665.

Rui, J., and R. Heijungs. 2010. "Industrial Ecosystems as a Social Network." In . Delft University of Technology; The Hague University of Applied Sciences; TNO. https://repository.tudelft.nl/view/conferencepapers/uuid:d93296a0-fd72-4f22-b3a2-1a8e0d80f003.

Singh, Nitish, Boris P. Bartikowski, Yogesh K. Dwivedi, and Miachael D. Williams. 2009. "Global Megatrends and the Web: Convergence of Globalization, Networks and Innovation." *ACM SIGMIS Database: The DATABASE for Advances in Information Systems* 40 (4): 14–27.

Singh, Rajesh, H.R. Murty, S.K. Gupta, and A. Dikshit. 2007. "Development of Composite Sustainability Performance Index for Steel Industry." *Ecological Indicators* 7 (July): 565–88. https://doi.org/10.1016/j.ecolind.2006.06.004.

Skivko, Maria. 2021. "Digital Technologies, Social Entrepreneurship and Governance for Sustainable Development." *Research in Social Change* 13 (1): 165–73. https://doi.org/10.2478/rsc-2021-0016.

Sommer, Klaus H. 2020. *Study and Portfolio Review of the Projects on Industrial Symbiosis in DG Research and Innovation: Findings and Recommendations.* Publications Office of the European Union Luxemburg. https://op.europa.eu/en/publication-detail/-/publication/f26dfd11-6288-11ea-b735-01aa75ed71a1.

Spender, John-Christopher, Vincenzo Corvello, Michele Grimaldi, and Pierluigi Rippa. 2017. "Startups and Open Innovation: A Review of the Literature." *European Journal of Innovation Management* 20 (1): 4–30. https://doi.org/10.1108/EJIM-12-2015-0131.

Stec, Małgorzata, and Mariola Grzebyk. 2018. "The Implementation of the Strategy Europe 2020 Objectives in European Union Countries: The Concept Analysis and Statistical Evaluation." *Quality & Quantity* 52 (1): 119–33.

Staff, Town, and Thomas Eddington. 2020. "Special Meeting." https://www.utah.gov/pmn/files/662195.pdf.

Stiglitz, Joseph E., and Justin Lin Yifu. 2013. *The Industrial Policy Revolution I: The Role of Government Beyond Ideology.* 2013° edizione. Basingstoke: Palgrave Macmillan.

Stocker, Thomas. 2014. *Climate Change 2013: The Physical Science Basis: Working Group I Contribution to the Fifth Assessment Report of the Intergovernmental Panel on Climate Change.* Cambridge university press. . https://www.ipcc.ch/report/ar5/wg1/.

Sum, Ngai-Ling, and Bob Jessop. 2013. *Towards a Cultural Political Economy: Putting Culture in Its Place in Political Economy.* Cheltenham, UK, Northampton, MA, USA: Edward Elgar Publishing. https://www.e-elgar.com/shop/gbp/towards-a-cultural-political-economy-9781783472437.html.

Tagliapietra, Simone, and Reinhilde Veugelers. 2020. "A Green Industrial Policy for Europe." *Bruegel Blueprint Series*, 2020.

Tosdevin, Annalisa. 2020. "European Commission Unveils Strategy for Shaping Europe's Digital Future." 2020. https://www.lexology.com/library/detail.aspx?g=bfe1dd00-5c96-4ec6-86ba-e7402b1bc21e.

Trading Economics. 2022. "Competitiveness Rank - Countries - List." Competitiveness Index. 2022. https://tradingeconomics.com/country-list/competitiveness-rank.

United Nations. 2015. "A/RES/70/1 Resolution Adopted by the General Assembly on 25 September 2015," October. https://www.un.org/en/development/desa/population/migration/generalassembly/docs/globalcompact/A_RES_70_1_E.pdf.

Vrande, Vareska van de, Jeroen P.J. de Jong, Wim Vanhaverbeke, and Maurice de Rochemont. 2009. "Open Innovation in SMEs: Trends, Motives and

Management Challenges." *Technovation* 29 (6–7): 423–37. https://doi.org/10.1016/j.technovation.2008.10.001.

Wade, Robert H. 2012. "Return of Industrial Policy?" *International Review of Applied Economics* 26 (2): 223–39. https://doi.org/10.1080/02692171.2011.640312.

Wautelet, Thibaut. 2020. "The Concept of Circular Economy: Its Origins and Its Evolutions." https://www.researchgate.net/publication/322555840_The_Concept_of_Circular_Economy_its_Origins_and_its_Evolution/link/5a5fcd1a458515b4377b840c/download.

West, Joel, and Marcel Bogers. 2014. "Leveraging External Sources of Innovation: A Review of Research on Open Innovation: Leveraging External Sources of Innovation." *Journal of Product Innovation Management* 31 (4): 814–31. https://doi.org/10.1111/jpim.12125.

West, Joel, and Marcel Bogers. 2017. "Open Innovation: Current Status and Research Opportunities." *Innovation* 19 (1): 43–50. https://doi.org/10.1080/14479338.2016.1258995.

West, Joel, Ammon Salter, Wim Vanhaverbeke, and Henry Chesbrough. 2014. "Open Innovation: The next Decade." *Research Policy* 43 (5): 805–11. https://doi.org/10.1016/j.respol.2014.03.001.

Winans, Kiara, Alissa Kendall, and Hui Deng. 2017. "The History and Current Applications of the Circular Economy Concept." *Renewable and Sustainable Energy Reviews* 68: 825–33. https://doi.org/10.1016/j.rser.2016.09.123.

Worldbank. 2022. "World Development Indicators | DataBank." 2022. https://databank.worldbank.org/reports.aspx?source=world-development-indicators#.

Wüst, Charlotte, and Nicky Rogge. 2022. "How Is the European Union Progressing towards Its Europe 2020 Targets? A Benefit-of-the-Doubt Window Analysis." *Empirica* 49 (2): 405–38.

Yilmaz, Ozge, Emre Yontem and Emrah Alkaya. 2016. "Industrial Symbiosis Indicators." http://fissacproject.eu/wp-content/uploads/2018/10/FISSAC_D1.6_Indicators_P11_16092016_FINAL.pdf.

About the Authors

Tamara Besednjak Valič is a senior scientific associate at the Rudolfovo - Science and Technology Centre Novo mesto and associate professor of sociology at the Faculty of Information Studies and School of Advanced Social Studies (Slovenia). Her research interests include innovation, university-industry collaboration, technology transfer and regional development.

Victor Cepoi is an assistant professor of sociology at the Faculty of Information Studies and the School of Advanced Social Studies (Slovenia). His research interests are regional development, innovation, social networks, and general and political trust.

Erika Džajić Uršič is a scientific associate at the Rudolfovo - Science and Technology Centre Novo mesto and assistant professor of social science informatics at the Faculty of Information Studies and School of Advanced Social Studies (Slovenia). Her research effort is on various aspects of social networks and behaviours in sustainable development, eco-industrial development and regional geography.

Urška Fric is an assistant professor of information studies at the Faculty of Information
Studies in Novo mesto and a scientific associate at the Rudolfovo - Science and Technology
Centre Novo mesto (Slovenia). Her research focuses on industrial symbiosis and analyses the structuration of industrial symbiosis networks. In recent years she has also researched intellectual property and knowledge and technologies transfer between research institutions and industries.

Cristian Gangaliuc is an assistant with a doctorate in sociology at the Faculty of Information Studies in Novo Mesto (Slovenia). His doctoral research and areas of interest include innovation, regional development and transnational value chains. He analysed regional innovation systems in EU and non-EU subnational regions focusing on endogenous and erogenous factors.

Alenka Pandiloska Jurak is a scientific associate at the Rudolfovo - Science and Technology Centre Novo mesto and an assistant professor of sociology at the Faculty of Information Studies in Novo Mesto and at the School of Advanced

Social Studies (Slovenia). Her research includes public policy analysis and analysis of networks established between the public and private sectors.

Borut Rončević is a senior research fellow at the Rudolfovo - Science and Technology Centre Novo mesto and professor of sociology at the Faculty of Information Studies, School of Advanced Social Studies (Slovenia). His main research interests are innovations and technologies in regional development, circular economy and socio-cultural factors of development.